DANTE

BY

JEFFERSON BUTLER FLETCHER

WITH AN INTRODUCTION BY

MARK MUSA

UNIVERSITY OF NOTRE DAME PRESS : 1965

CONTENTS

INTRODUCTION

In "The War and the Professor of Literature," an essay published the same year as *Dante*, Jefferson Butler Fletcher (1865–1946) voiced the need for critical perspective:

> We shall need more than ever both eyes of the mind—the eye of understanding and the eye of imagination. It takes two eyes, I believe, to see things in the round. The one eye of him who has learning without imagination reports only surfaces.

Dante certainly saw "things in the round." And Fletcher's book is an attempt, a successful effort, to see Dante in that way: with both eyes of the mind, the understanding he accumulated as a research scholar and professor at Harvard and Columbia, and the imagination he displayed in his essays and articles and often in his own poetry.

So many critics of Dante approach his works along a single, narrow path; their critical journey is either entirely philosophical, or theological, or political, or aesthetic, or sometimes exclusively emotional. But to travel such a path can, at best, lead only to a categorized appreciation of the poet's art. The fastidious Dante scholarship— that meticulous research, the compiling of footnotes into voluminous commentary, during the latter part of the nineteenth century by the scholars who read Dante's poetry as a kind of autobiographical account in code—was certainly necessary and valuable. True, Dante's private

life does invade his writings, and there is some truth in
Charles Eliot Norton's statement that "it is needful to
know Dante as man in order fully to appreciate him as
poet." But Dante, unlike Rousseau or Byron, reveals to
his reader only that much of himself which may serve
as an example to other men; he will display only that
much of himself which he considers necessary for his
purpose; and to probe his innermost private life, as
many critics would have us do, will at best satisfy curiosity but will never bring us closer to an understanding
of his poetry. Dante is not writing a diary; rather, as
St. Augustine in The Confessions, he is concerned with
universalizing himself, that is, when he presents his case,
he presents the case for all men—the case of every man.
The main action of Dante's drama reveals how God
drew him unto Himself through a woman, Beatrice, and
Dante's purpose in revealing his drama is to show that
God can do the same for every man.

Fletcher, then, objects vehemently to all those critics
who consider Dante's earliest poetic endeavor, the Vita
nuova, a "naïve diary." While some of his general statements concerning troubadour poetry and the so-called
school of the dolce stil nuovo may be somewhat over-
simplified, and at times ingenuous, he does have a number of fine insights into the Vita nuova, many of which
have been adopted and elaborated by Dante scholars of
our own day. Many scholars, however, still judge Dante
artistically immature at this early stage of his literary
career; they are still perplexed by the Vita nuova, and
continue to ask themselves why Dante went to such pains
to explain the obvious while at the same time he by-
passed that which was seemingly obscure. The Vita
nuova emerges as a very careful, thorough and dramatic
rendering of the poet's personal spiritual growth under
the direction of Love. Dante, it is true, expects a good

deal from his reader: attentiveness, alertness and, above all, willingness to learn ("Not one who runs can read him," says Fletcher, "but only one who lingers and meditates and looks before and after in the text"). To the reader of the *Vita nuova* (and certainly of the *Divina Comedia*), understanding comes slowly, gradually, by stages; and it must be so, for to Dante the poet it came precisely the same way. Fletcher is right in saying that "the *Vita nuova* is not an igenuous diary of the heart but a complex piece of literary goldsmith's art."

The author's references to St. Paul and St. Augustine are especially helpful in explaining Dante's main purpose, in particular the passage from St. Paul: "For now we see through a glass, darkly; but then face to face; now I know in part; but then shall I know even as also I am known," which Fletcher interprets as follows: "The inner truth of which his experience was but a running symbol or allegory written by God's hand, reached his sense-darkened mind at first only confusedly, then as veil after veil is lifted, with perfect clarity." In the *Vita nuova* Dante takes his reader through his own stages of learning—his three movements in love—to enlightenment, as he will do again, though more elaborately, in the *Divine Comedy*.

Fletcher's treatment of Dante's lesser-known works is impressive. The solutions he proposes for some of the complex problems of the *Convivio* are sound and convincing and very much in circulation today. The *De Vulgaria Eloquentia* (Dante's essay, *On Vernacular Eloquence*) fits easily into his general plan of things: as with the rest of his writings, it has a strong personal background; not only does it establish the principles others should work from, but also it sets forth Dante's own performance to be used as example or model. By interpreting Dante through his own writings the author of this little book succeeds in making a number of original and incisive observations. At one point Fletcher complains that while Dante, as any great poet, is sensitive to shades of fitness and style—the word and fact fitting tightly together—he nevertheless seems to do little to individualize the dialogue, and his invectives and outbursts are similar in tone whether it is Dante himself or a sinner who speaks. Comments such as this run throughout the book and are geared to make the reader pause and reflect, at times to object but always to react. Fletcher is particularly perceptive when talking about Dante's canzone and other lyrics: "There still clings about Dante's expression of sentiment something of the fastidiously conventional elegance of the troubadour, about his expression of thought something of the argumentative subtlety of the schoolman." This is certainly true of the canzone (perhaps even less true of the sonnets and ballate), and the one that opens the Fourth Book of the Convivio is the first to come to mind; Fletcher thinks of it in terms of a rhyming disquisition, like Pope's Essay on Man!

The appeal of the Divine Comedy, unlike a good many of the lyrics, is not aristocratic, exclusive, for an in-group, but rather it is universal; the poem is for every man— according to Dante it is written in a "lax and humble" style which best suits the genre of comedy—with a precise purpose in mind, "to remove those living in this life from the state of misery and lead them to the state of felicity," as Dante says in his letter to Can Grande.

In discussing the Hell, Fletcher does not fail to comment on the standard, distinguished and tragic figures such as Francesca, Ulysses and Count Ugoline; but, happily enough, he is also aware of a less frequently publicized feature of the Underworld—its humor. Not all of his illustrations are equally convincing: it is indeed difficult to think of the contest between the avaricious and

the prodigal as a shoving contest with a comic suggestion of modern "push-ball"; on the other hand, there is
a grotesque humor at play in the invention of many of
the infernal demons and guardians, and one is tempted
to smile at Minos with his convenient "index" tail.

While the torments imposed on the penitents in the
Purgatory are certainly no less grotesque than those in
Hell, Dante shifts the focus of attention from the suffering he describes to a mood of brotherly love, of friendly
meetings and reunions, climaxed by Dante's reunion with
Beatrice in the earthly paradise. In *Hell* Dante's mind
was bent on matters of fact, on the sinners and their
punishments, and there is no high speculative discourse;
in the *Purgatory*, however, many questions are raised
concerning moral responsibility and the tone is one of
repentance.

Throughout his book Fletcher discusses the *Paradise*
as much poetically as in light of the important part it
plays in the over-all structure and purpose of the *Divine
Comedy*; he realizes that it presents a difficult artistic
problem to Dante. Finally, toward the close of his third
chapter—as though it had been all the while in the back
of his poetical mind—Fletcher with sensitivity and good
taste puts into words that which must certainly disturb
many a student of Dante who attempts to read the entire
Comedy with "both eyes of the mind":

> . . . it is matter for infinite regret, I feel, that the artist who
> made Francesca live, and Piccarda, and the young Beatrice,
> should so cloud his poet's vision as to see his sweet lady at the
> last but as a glorified scholastic doctor. . . . To my thinking,
> this pedanticizing of Beatrice is the "spot on the sun" of the
> *Paradise*. In it, the theologian has shouldered out the poet.

Believing that Dante, and also St. Augustine, were concerned above all with giving "example and instruction"

to all men, Fletcher divides his chapters into (I) "Dante's Personal Confessions" (experience as example); (II) "Dante's Impersonal Teaching"; (III) "Dante's Literary Art" (echoing Dante in his tripartite division). At the close of his brief introduction Fletcher comments: "Thus, by example making for goodness, by instruction declaring truth, by art producing beauty, his message in its three aspects fitly expresses the ideal trinity of him whom Dante is spiritually the avatar—Plato, subtle logician and maker of beautiful myths."

Fletcher never loses sight of "the dominant virtue of Dante's art": the interpenetration of the sensuous and the significant—the fusion of the theologian and poet, of poetry and thought. *Dante* is thus a book of broad perspective. It is almost as if this critic imitates Dante in directing understanding and imagination toward a vision of more than single dimension.

MARK MUSA
Indiana University
Bloomington, Ind.
April 1, 1965

CHAPTER I

DANTE'S PERSONAL CONFESSIONS

CHAPTER I

Dante's Personal Confessions

"And the Lord said unto me, Behold, I have put my words into thy mouth." Jeremiah, I, 9.

I

THE NEW LIFE

DANTE'S first confession—in St. Augustine's sense of the word—is the *New Life*. In a brief preface he promises to give the *sentenzia*, or signification, of what he calls his new life. This new life began with his first sight of Beatrice in his ninth year. From then on, he declares, he was obedient to that impulse of love, though twice misunderstanding its guidance he twice offended his lady. The first of these misunderstandings occurred during her lifetime, when prompted by love to disguise his service of her he simulated love for two other ladies in succession. The second misunderstanding occurred after her death, when for a time he was moved actually to love a gentle lady who had shown compassion for his forlornness. For each of these errors retribution was prompt. His peace of mind was broken by a "battle of thoughts";

the bliss of Beatrice's salutation was withheld from him; until, humbled and contrite, he received again through her mercy forgiveness and new peace. At the last, consoled by dreamed-of salutation of her in heaven, he dedicated himself to such loving-service here on earth as might merit her actual salutation hereafter where she "gazeth in glory on the face of him, *qui est per omnia saecula benedictus.*"

Dante tells his story on the basis of poems ostensibly written on certain actual and crucial occasions. In prose he paraphrases, connects, and interprets these poems as one who has come to recognize the direction and goal of his total experience. In this first book, he says later, "I spoke before entering upon my youth."[1] The statement holds only of the poems,—indeed rigorously only of the poems written before Beatrice's death in 1290; for then reaching his twenty-fifth year, he entered upon his "youth"—as that age was reckoned. It was these occasional poems that truly and spontaneously expressed him in that earlier time of "adolescence"; and such expression is what he probably meant by the words "I spoke." The *New Life* as a whole, however, in which the thirty odd poems constituting the "original record" of his love-experience are digested by retrospective judgment, cannot have been composed until at least three or four years after Beatrice's death, when Dante would be nearing thirty. The fact is sufficient rebuttal of the not infrequent assumption that the *New Life* must be regarded as boyishly naïve and immature.

The promised significance of Dante's new life is shown to be redemption through love. But love, they say, is blind. How shall the blind lead the blind? Is there indeed a love not blind, obedient to which blind man may attain his longed-for end,—the stilling of desire which is peace?

[1] *Banquet*, I, i, 125–7.

Dante does—and must—premise such a discerning love, and defines it formally in the sonnet beginning—

> Love and the gentle heart are one same thing,
> As saith the Sage.[2]

This definition of love underlies Dante's whole self-interpretation. For it he frankly here and elsewhere[3] admits obligation to Guido Guinicelli, of whose famous *canzone* on the "gentle heart" Dante's sonnet is a virtual summary. It will be useful to consider the doctrine of the poet whom Dante affectionately called "father of me and of my betters."[4]

To put the matter in a word, Guinicelli made Italian "troubadour" poetry sincere. Sincerity, as Dante told Bonagiunta da Lucca on the Mount of Purgatory,[5] was the single "knot" that held back the older "Sicilian" school, of which Bonagiunta is made representative, from that of the "sweet new style" fathered by Guinicelli.

The Sicilian school, so called by Dante himself,[6] takes its name from the court of the Emperor Frederick II, who was also King of the Two Sicilies. In his court, refugees from Provence, devastated by the Albigensian Crusade of 1208–18, found protection. Among these refugees were troubadours, whose poetry became fashionable at the brilliant and cosmopolitan court; and soon Frederick himself, his son Enzo, and his minister, Pier delle Vigne, set august example of imitating it in Italian.

This imitation of the Provençal lyric of courtly love was the first Italian poetry to be composed with conscious literary art. Its influence was immediate. Frederick held court not only in Sicily proper, but also in southern Italy.

---

[2] *New Life*, son. x.   [3] *Banquet*, IV, xx.
[4] *Purg.*, xxvi, 97–8.   [5] *Purg.*, xxiv, 49 ff.
[6] ". . . quicquid poetantur Itali Sicilianum vocatur . . ." *On Vernacular Eloquence*, I, xii, 8–9.

Thence the fashion of the new poetry spread northward. In its native tongue it was already known in North Italy, where Provençal poets had visited during the twelfth century. It had found imitators, notably Sordello of Mantua, to whom Dante paid such high homage. But these imitators, feeling their own vernacular to be raw and uncouth, had used Provençal. Now that the Sicilians had shown the possibilities of Italian, educated townsmen everywhere turned to it. Proficiency in the new art was evidence of patriotism no less than of culture.

The defect of this lyric outburst was, as Dante said, its insincerity. Neither Frederick's courtiers nor the burghers of the towns meant, or could mean, what they sang. The motive of Provençal love-poetry was feudal homage to high-born ladies. The poet was most often a servitor of the house as well as of the heart. Whether fact or feigning, his passion was controlled in act and expression by a rigid code of genteel conventions. Usually, the real boon he sought was neither the lady's hand—she was generally married—nor her honor, but such condescending favor as a great lord might bestow upon a deserving vassal. There were occasional exceptions, when the genteel homage masked illicit intrigue.

In a sense, it is hardly fair to call the Provençal troubadours insincere. They were frankly venal,—though it must be said they paid for maintenance by an art formally exquisite. And their courtier obsequiousness was, if often extravagant, at least not incongruous in a society where caste ruled and elegant women were in the ascendant. In the semi-oriental Sicilian court and in the democratic communes, on the other hand, the elaborately abject posturing of the troubadour lover was altogether out of keeping with real life. Frederick kept a harem guarded by eunuchs. Women had no standing in his court. If the town poets, on the other hand—chiefly

notaries, magistrates, clerics—had really tried to live up
to their poetical professions, they would only have been
laughed at for their pains,—as Dante admits he was
laughed at by Beatrice and her girl-friends. "Sicilian"
lyric love was therefore mere literary posing, untrue to
actual life,—and this whether or not the poet happened
to be really in love.

Writing a generation before Dante, Guido Guinicelli
of Bologna, university man and magistrate, by amending
the troubadour code of love in a single but fundamental
particular, made it true to Italian ideals of life.

> Love and the gentle heart are one same thing,

Dante makes him say. Verbally, it is but reaffirmation of
the Provençal axiom that love, properly speaking, is the
affair solely of gentlefolk. For by gentility the troubadour meant social caste. Guinicelli made it mean personal character. The true lover need not be a gentleman;
he must be a *gentle* man.

> Let no man predicate
> That ought the name of gentleness should have,
> Even in a king's estate,
> Except the heart there be a gentle man's.[7]

In Rossetti's translation two words are ignored that fix
the meaning more exactly. Guinicelli says gentility must
come "*da virtute*," from virtue. The true lover is the virtuous man, loving not by genteel code of caste, but by
gentle code of character. In other words, Guinicelli spirit-
ualized the feudal chivalric conventions of love; and so
inaugurated a new and nobler Italian poetry, the so-called
"sweet new style." Intimations of Guinicelli's idea occur
here and there in poems of his precursors; but it was he

[7] *Canzone, Of the Gentle Heart*, ll. 35–8.

who saw and brilliantly realized the possibilities of the idea. And Dante's own warm-hearted acknowledgment of Guinicelli's leadership is sufficient answer to the critical scrupulosity which, on the ground of these scattered anticipations of detail, has questioned Guinicelli's originality.

Love, according to Guinicelli, is not merely peculiar to the gentle, or virtuous, heart. The whole virtue of such a heart is love. A virtuous disposition is one disposed to love. Love is the expression of a virtuous disposition. And that which incites the virtuous disposition to express itself is beauty:

> And so the heart created by God's breath
> Pure, true, and clean from guile,
> A woman, like a Star, enamoreth.[8]

All desire is for something we have not. The beauty, therefore, which awakens desire in the gentle heart is a beauty not already possessed by it, yet to which, once seen, it aspires. Obviously, the beauty that can enamor the gentle heart must itself be gentle. This was, as we have seen, axiomatic in the troubadour code. But now translated into ethical terms, it means that a virtuous soul yearns to a virtue unpossessed. When at the close of his *canzone* Guinicelli pleads before God the inevitableness of his love for one who

> . . . had the likeness of an angel
> That was of Thy kingdom,

he sums up in principle his whole doctrine. It was the angelic, the divine, in his lady's beauty that drew to itself his virtuous desire as fatally as magnet the iron-filing. The gentle lover loves his lady because she is indeed

----

[8] *Of the Gentle Heart,* ll. 18–20.

made in the image of God,—and in that degree. She is a mirror in which God shows somewhat of himself in order to win a soul. And

> The like in woman worketh worthy man,

adds Dante in his summarizing sonnet.

This adoration of God reflected for each in each is holy love, charity, in the highest. So shall the blessed love in heaven,—only beholding God face to face as well as by mutual reflection of him. And so is more richly meaningful the young Dante's declaration that when Beatrice "appeared from any direction, by the hope of her wondrous salutation no enemy was left to me, but rather a flame of charity[9] possessed me which made me pardon whomsoever had offended me; and to him who had then asked of me concerning any matter, my answer would have been simply: *Love!* with a countenance clothed in humility."[10] The purport of the *New Life* is to show how in his own case this high mood of love, at first transitory, inhibited by blind impulses of his unregenerate human nature, became at last by the grace of God permanent.

The seeming egotism of such assurance vanishes on recognition that Dante would glorify not himself but God. Divine love is the protagonist of the drama, ever in actual dream or by mental suggestion guiding Dante. God's meaning itself is never obscure; but as a cup, though the sea be poured into it, yet receives no more than a cupful, so Dante receives God's messages only in the measure of his own understanding. To his imperfect understanding Divine Love appears as a dread figure in a fiery cloud, strangely feeding to the lady Beatrice her

[9] In the theological sense,—holy love.
[10] *New Life*, xi, 1–9.

lover's burning heart; as a pilgrim, tattered and torn, bidding Dante simulate love for another than his true lady; as a youth in white raiment enigmatically warning Dante of unlikeness to him, "the lord of nobleness," and bidding Dante turn back from those simulated loves to his true lady. Later, as it seems, Love, now joyous, compares the approach of Beatrice, preceded as she is by the lady Joan, with the coming of Christ, preceded by the man John, and also identifies Beatrice with himself— "because of great likeness." And accordingly in Dante's next following vision, Love appears in his true likeness, Beatrice—returned from the grave to recall her apostate lover from his new false love. At last, transported in mind to the paradise of divine love itself, he sees her suffused with the very glory of that love.

Thus is the true identity of the enigmatic visitant of his dreams and inspirations finally revealed as God himself. Through loving, Dante has come to the understanding of love. And from the height of such understanding, looking backward over the way, he can see how guidance has been ever given by and towards God. Even his blind stumblings and fallings away have been made by God's mercy means of spiritual progress. To his humbled and contrite heart God had said as to Paul: "My grace is sufficient for thee: for my strength is made perfect in weakness."[11] Therefore like Paul, Dante will glory not of himself, but in his infirmities.

Because the motive of the New Life is a confession of God in the spirit of St. Paul, this not in the least proves the love-story itself a fiction. On the contrary, only by confession of actual experience could Dante offer that "sure testimony" which he says justified St. Paul and St. Augustine in speaking of themselves before men. As fiction, the New Life might still

[11] *II Cor.*, xii, 9.

> assert eternal Providence,
> And justify the ways of God to men.

Assertion and justification, however, would be merely theoretic, not proved by example. Dante's apology for speaking of himself would be mere dramatic feigning. This of course is possible. All the evidences we have, however, point the other way. The circumstantial detail, the coincidences—close enough for mystery, yet inexact enough for verisimilitude, the allusions of contemporaries—such as Cino's consoling *canzone* after Beatrice's death, Boccaccio's direct testimony,—these things and others incline us to believe Dante's story. That he should moralize—even allegorize—it, is no impeachment of its truth. For him all reality is symbolic; the higher allegory is only the inner truth of reality.

Confusion on this point is source of much misunderstanding. The modern reader is puzzled by the *New Life*. He finds no plain unvarnished tale, but one overlaid with enigmas and insinuations, an author at often tedious pains to explain the obvious, yet either passing over really obscure matters in silence or, seeming to explain, only adding obscurity to obscurity. He may feel the lofty idealism, the tender beauty of particular passages, the emotional intensity—perhaps here and there too intense for modern taste; but he may judge Dante as yet artistically immature, or perhaps youthfully given to modishness and mystification. One German critic attributes to such traits the particular appeal of the *New Life* to all aesthetes.[12]

It may be admitted that the plan of the *New Life* is in some aspects a "dark conceit." But the enigmatic manner is due neither to immature clumsiness nor to literary

[12] Karl Vossler: *Die göttliche Komödie*, Heidelberg, 1907, p. 516.

affectation. It is rather a carefully thought out attempt to render dramatically the gradual process of Dante's own spiritual enlightenment under the guidance of love. In the course of the experience related he passed in relative degree from the first to the second grade of spiritual insight indicated by St. Paul: "For now we see through a glass, darkly (according to the Vulgate—*in aenigmate*); but then face to face: now I know in part; but then shall I know even as also I am known."[13] In other words, the inner truth of which his experience was but a running symbol or allegory written by God's hand, reached his sense-darkened mind at first only confusedly, then, as veil after veil is lifted, with perfect clarity. He would have his reader pass through the stages of his enlightenment with him. So to the thoughtful reader the *New Life* clears as it goes,—but the reader must be a thoughtful one.

Again, if from the very outset in the love dominating his life there was something sacred,—something that grew clearer as his insight cleared, must not that divine influence have colored the songs he had written at the dictation of love? For as he was to define his poetry,

> I am one who, when Love
> Inspires me, note, and in the way that he
> Dictates within, I give the outward form.[14]

If it was indeed God who spoke to him as love, must not his own echoing words render God's message in the degree of his human understanding? And might he not now, having reached fuller understanding of God, interpret these songs, notes taken from love's dictation as they were, anew and with new lights—just as his Virgil, returned from the other world of enlightenment, might

[13] *I Cor.*, xiii, 12.   [14] *Purg.*, xxiv, 52–4.

have told the other shades in Limbo how all unwittingly
he had prophesied in his fourth eclogue the future Christ?

So, reviewing his past in memory and in poems record-
ing intimate experience, Dante finds manifold signs and
premonitions of supernatural guidance. Design seems
now to lie in the common root of his lady's name, Beatrice, and the word "beatitude" for the heavenly reward
of the Christian. Had not love at once taught him to find
his beatitude in her salutation? And his very word for
"salutation"—*salute*—means in Italian "salvation" also.
So in her salvation in heaven is his eternal beatitude, for
she has drawn and will draw him to her there. The persistent recurrence of "nine" in the numbering of the year
or day or hour when her influence decisively swayed him
was God's way of associating her influence with his own;
for the root of nine is three, the Trinity. So when Dante
had been moved to sing of meeting Joan, also called
Primavera, followed by Beatrice, and he had made Love
say—

> This is Primavera,
> And her whose name is Love, so me she mirrors,—

he could not then see as now the analogy with that other
John, who "*prima verrà*"—"will come first," or before
Christ; and Christ is Love—as Beatrice is for Dante
Love's counterpart.

Still more manifestly yet darkly premonitory are the
seven visions vouchsafed him, like St. Paul,[15] at crucial
moments. To analyze these in detail would be out of scale
in this essay. They have, however, a common principle.
Dante ostensibly relates each vision just as it occurred.
To him at the time of its occurrence its meaning had
been enigmatic. So to the reader who has progressed
only thus far in the story its meaning is equally enig-

[15] *Cf.* II Cor., xii.

matic. But to the degree that, enlightened by the outcome, Dante gradually understands, the reader also is
let into the secret. The visions, in short, are ambiguous
oracles, dark in the present, clear in the retrospect. The
obscurity was not in the message dictated, but in the re-
ceiving mind. Accordingly, the later visions are in themselves clearer, because Dante's insight has cleared.

Again the question arises as to Dante's sincerity. Has
he merely read back into his love-poems these prophetic
intimations and revelations as Tasso, for instance, read
a moral allegory into his *Jerusalem Delivered* after it
was already written, or as medieval commentators allegorized Virgil or Ovid? Again, possibly. But if so, again
the "sure testimony" of his personal confession would be
to that extent impeached. And why should we doubt?

Dante was a mystic, for whom direct communication
between God and men is an article of faith. St. Augustine, the precedent of whose *Confessions* he follows, had
said in them: "Woe is me! and dare I say that Thou
heldest Thy peace, O my God, while I wandered further
from Thee? Didst Thou then indeed hold Thy peace to
me? And whose but Thine were these words which by
my mother, Thy faithful one, Thou sangest in my
ears?"[16] So through Love God had sung in Dante's
ears,—Love later identified with Beatrice, also God's
"faithful one" and in Paradise Dante's spiritual mother.[17]
The definition of his poetic vocation thus takes on a
richer literalness. When he says—

> I am one who, when Love
> Inspires me, note, and in the way that he
> Dictates within, I give the outward form,

he means literally just what he says. In his poems he
has declared what God through Love, incarnate in Bea-

[16] Bk. II, par. 7. Pusey's translation.   [17] Cf. *Par.*, xxii, 1–6.

trice, had dictated within his heart, even though he had not realized the full import of the inspiration he noted and expressed. He had been as Nebuchadnezzar telling his dream; later he was become the Daniel to interpret that dream to himself and others.

The *New Life* still leaves the full import of his experience uninterpreted,—or at least not explicitly interpreted. Although in fact well aware of that import, Dante maintains in the book the dramatic rôle of the dreamer who is not yet also the seer. The *dramatic* "time" of the *New Life* was, as we have seen, his adolescence, when most of the experiences related took place. In his adolescence, as he says, be "began to perceive many things as in a dream; as may be seen in the *New Life*,"[18] —that is, his actual new life, which was also his young life.[19]

II

THE BANQUET

WHATEVER the date of composition of the *Banquet*, its dramatic time is, as Dante says, over that threshold of maturity yet uncrossed by the spokesman of the *New Life*. Entered upon the age of wisdom, he would now, he says, speak of his experience no longer as the youth dreaming dreams, but as the man knowing what his past dreams signify by the translation of them into action. He will declare the Wisdom of God which has been revealed to him. That is the larger reason for his again speaking of himself. There is, however, another reason.

People have mistaken his poetic confessions for mere vain and amatorious passion. To vindicate himself, as

[18] *Banquet*, II, xiii, 27–9.
[19] The word *nuova* has this alternative meaning.

well as the divine Wisdom whose dictation he had but
noted down in them according to his lights, Dante will
declare the true meaning of certain *canzoni*, or odes, of
love.

He promised to interpret fourteen of these, but for reasons unexplained actually discussed but three. From allusions in the text, and from contemporary manuscript
lists of the fourteen odes, we can plausibly identify and
order the other eleven, all of which are extant. The work
as it stands, however, is not a fragment in the usual
sense. For it gives fully and integrally the promised vindication of one misunderstood episode of love in Dante's
experience. This was the episode following Beatrice's
death, when, as he tells in the *New Life*, his heart was
won by a gentle lady who showed compassion for his forlorn state. Having vindicated to his own satisfaction that
affair, Dante breaks off. A later and seemingly more serious entanglement, however, is implied in a set of im-
passioned odes addressed to one called now the Maiden,
la Pargoletta, now the Stone, *la Pietra*. Explanation of
these strongly sensuous poems as dictations of divine
Wisdom would seem less easy than of the chastely ideal-
izing praises of the Compassionate Lady, yet Dante was
bound in consistency to attempt such an explanation.
How he might have succeeded will be discussed later.

As its title implies, the *Banquet* was to offer some
gathered fragments of the "food of angels," wisdom, as
well as to hold up Dante's experience of love as an edifying example. So by a characteristically medieval method,
Dante made the work almost an encyclopedia. By extended definition of terms and other lengthy digression,
he introduced a great variety of miscellaneous information. Why he broke off we do not know. His method, indeed, does not commend itself to modern taste. Possible
interest in the main argument, abstract and difficult as

it is, is thwarted by the constant digressions. The medieval appetite, however, was more hearty. It particularly relished such a mixed repast of dictionary and encyclopedia, sermon and romance. Giovanni Villani in his Florentine chronicle says of the *Banquet*,—"This commentary, to judge by what we have of it, would have been a lofty, beautiful, subtle, and very great work."[20] At least it gives us invaluable helps to the fixing of Dante's ideas and habits of thought in general, and—more importantly—explains how he ingeniously turned to edification even his more dubious experiences and writings. He will indeed, following St. Paul, glory in his infirmities. On the surface, to be sure, he seems to admit no fault. In this second work are none of the tears and agonizings of contrition of the *New Life*. He would write as becomes a man, temperately and rationally. He will coolly explain, not emotionally appeal.

He begins by startling us with the assertion that his second love, the Compassionate Lady, is just Philosophy. We naturally feel that a vindication on such lines must only add insolence to guilt. Critics have shaken their heads over the great man's moment of disingenuous weakness, applying Virgil's words—

"Let us not speak of *that*; but look and pass!"

Others indeed have done what Dante seems to be doing. Torquato Tasso, for instance, later explained away as allegory the love-stories in his epic. But are we quite sure that we have understood Dante in this matter? Personally, I think we have not; and I mean to propose—as best I may in a brief and nontechnical study—an alternative reading of his self-vindication.

The argument of the *Banquet* differs from that of the

[20] Bk. ix, chap. 136.

New Life only in that Dante now declares the true meaning of his poems explicitly, instead of by enigmatic implication. His second work really supplements his first. "I do not mean," he says, "to derogate that work in any part, but rather to support it by this."[21]

In fine, he means to say again, and this time clearly—as befits one who has crossed the threshold of manhood,—that his wooing of the Compassionate Lady was as much at the dictation of true love as his wooing of Beatrice, and should have involved no disloyalty to Beatrice. If temporarily he had been in act disloyal, it was no fault of the love that moved him, but of his own incapacity to understand its dictates.

The same deity had inspired his odes to his second love whom in the first vision of the *New Life* he had seen as one in a fiery cloud, dread yet gladsome, who had fed to Beatrice her lover's burning heart and then carried her away with him heavenward. Now the simplest can understand that vision.[22] God had made Beatrice carry away the desire of his heart with her to heaven,—as later she herself will tell him.[23]

By God's will Beatrice was leading Dante to glory. But there is one glory of heaven, and another glory of earth. One way indeed—the narrow way of obedience to God's will—leads through the earthly glory to the heavenly; but the journey is in two stages. Two guides therefore are needful. Beatrice was to lead Dante to the ultimate goal of eternal glory in heaven; the Compassionate Lady, as it turned out, set him in the way towards the nearer goal of true earthly glory,—no less true for being temporal and passing. She was the providential agency by which God had won him to return to his appointed task in life when desperate for loss of Bea-

[21] *Banquet*, I, i, 114–6.   [22] *New Life*, iii, 105–7.
[23] *Purg.*, xxxi, 22–4.

trice. She properly was no more Beatrice's rival than mankind's one guide, the Emperor, was properly rival of its other, the Pope.

When Beatrice had died, Dante in passionate grief had longed for his own death, that he might be reunited with her in heaven. But he was not ripe for heaven; and God had yet a task for him on earth. So the Compassionate Lady, unwittingly weaning his mind from the lost Beatrice and reconciling him with life, actually served God and saved Dante. Thus even because Dante had been infirm of faith towards Beatrice, by God's grace his very infirmity had been made his strength, and his power to rejoin her hereafter.

Thus also in effect his second love had done for him precisely what Philosophy is divinely designed to do. As there are two glories, two rewards of blessedness, set before man, the one temporal and the other eternal, so to him, as just said, are given two guides,—in abstract terms, reason and revelation. But it is not left to man's private and individual judgment to interpret these guides. There is an authorized interpreter of reason, or philosopher, and an authorized interpreter of revelation, or theologian. Aristotle is the philosopher whose doctrine is to be accepted, says Dante, as "virtually Catholic opinion." Following Aristotle's principles, man arrives at that perfectly moral life which is "the end for which man is ordained so far as he is man."[24] It is for the Pope as head of the Church, on the other hand, and as supreme theologian by divine right, to interpret revelation, and so by teaching a truly religious life here to prepare man for that end for which he is ordained as co-equal of the angels hereafter.

Dante then does not mean—as has been too often assumed—to get rid of his question-raising second love by

[24] *Banquet*, IV, vi.

dissolving her away into a mere allegorical abstraction. She is Philosophy only as, in the *Divine Comedy*, Beatrice is Theology. She was actually, like Beatrice, a human being whose influence had providentially set him in that path of felicity which is charted for all by philosophy and theology. Whether at the time he realized this, or whether either lady was ever conscious of her saving mission, is another story, and in the present connection unimportant. He would acknowledge the guidance of God, of whom these ladies were but instruments. Their beauty had drawn him into the way of salvation; once on that way, the divine wisdom expressed in inspired philosophy and theology had also opened to his mind the meaning of his homeward journey, and so increased his grateful love for the human instruments of Providence.

His second love was in function like Philosophy. Substituting like for like, he is enabled to turn description and praise of her in his odes into description and praise of Philosophy, or wisdom governing man's life on earth. The wisdom of the life to come, "the living Beatrice in bliss," is not denied in the *Banquet*, but properly declared to be outside its scope.[25] The wisdom of this present life, however, has two aspects, according as it enriches the mind or governs the will. In the first aspect it is right knowledge of the world; in the second, right power among men. At bottom each aspect involves the other. Knowledge is power, and the right exercise of power brings knowledge. *Experientia docet*. But we may choose to be students of life or actors in life. And right choice depends upon our individual capacity, as implanted by nature and the grace of God.

Dante says he will confine himself in the *Banquet* to the moral virtues, the practical aspect of wisdom, because "in every discipline heed should be given to the

[25] *Banquet*, II, ix, 51–136.

capacity of the learner, and he should be led by that path which is easiest to him."[26] And the average capacity is rather for the moral virtues than the intellectual.

In this particular passage Dante is speaking not personally, but generally; yet in a special sense the practical life was, as he came to learn, fitted to his own capacity. Dante certainly regarded himself as of more than average capacity; but he also believed himself directed to teach and to prophesy. If his mission in life was thus practical, his capacity must be also practical. God's appointments are not perverse like those of men, who into religion force one born to the sword, and of the born preacher make a king.[27]

The same words by which at Love's dictation he had declared allegiance to the Compassionate Lady, also, as it turned out, declared for him his calling. It was, he had said, the Intelligences moving the third heaven that, speaking in his heart, had dictated his desire. These Intelligences, "natured[28] by the Holy Spirit," inspire love according to the capacity of the one inspired. And the love they actually inspired in him led him, as he says, to "the loving practice of Wisdom," l'amoroso uso della Sapientia,—that is, to the

> Virtue that giveth man felicity
> In his activity.[29]

By implication, then, his capacity was for the active life. In fact, shortly after the triumph of the Compassionate Lady over him, he assumed the full responsibilities of Florentine citizenship. According to indications in the New Life and the Banquet the episode of the

[26] Banquet, IV, xvii, 120–3.   [27] Cf. Par., viii, 115–48.
[28] Naturati, i.e. endowed with the quality of the Holy Spirit. Cf. Banquet, II, vi, 110.
[29] Ib., Canz., iii, 83–4. Cf. Ib., IV, ii, 153.

Compassionate Lady would extend from 1291 to 1294 or
1295.[30] In the latter year, or soon after, he married
Gemma Donati, daughter of an ancient and noble
Guelph family. Also, having reached the age of eligibil-
ity, he qualified for the higher state offices by enrolling
himself in the Guild of Physicians and Apothecaries,
one of the wealthiest and most important in Florence.
As reward of his political activity he was elected in 1300
one of the six Priors, chief officials of the city. Later in
the same year he was exiled. To that crucial year also
he assigned his moment of spiritual peril, lost in the
dark wood of error.

Not "felicity," but misery would then seem to have
been the immediate reward of his activity. So in the
New Life misery had followed upon his yielding to the
sway of the Compassionate Lady. "Gentle" she had
been, indeed in hue and feature like Beatrice,[31] love
of her had seemed "most noble";[32] yet the reward of
his desire was humiliation of spirit, and the desire itself,
as he had too late seen, culpable.[33] Yet the evil, to
speak rightly, was not in the fact of his desire, but in
its quality. To desire the Compassionate Lady as a solace for his true lady, gone where he might not yet follow, was a dictation of love ambiguous in import. To
find in her a consoling reminder of Beatrice was really
through her to feed his desire of Beatrice. To desire her,
the solace, for her very self was to be false to Beatrice.
In the New Life his confessed error was to have taken
the second alternative. In the Banquet he declared the
first alternative to be the right intention of Love's oracle. So in respect to his inspired call to the active life,
not because he had followed the inspiration, but because

[30] Cf. G. R. Carpenter in *Publ. Amer. Dante Soc.*, vol. VIII.
[31] *New Life*, xxxvii, 1–6.   [32] *Ib.*, xxxvi, 22–3.
[33] *Ib.*, xl, 14–15.

he had followed it in the wrong spirit, had he suffered exile and misery. The judgment of men had been indeed unjust. But the judgments of God are never unjust; and it was a chastening God who smote him through the injustice of men. For as he had desired the Compassionate Lady for herself, so he had desired earthly glory for itself. The motive of his activity had been self-love, worldly ambition.

> Half-way upon the journey of our life
> I roused to find myself within a forest
> In darkness, for the straight way had been lost.[34]

Had he but followed the right intention of Love's oracle, the true dictation of the angelic Intelligences, and valued earthly glory merely as the solacing reflection of heavenly glory, he would indeed have found a felicity that not even unjust exile could take away. He would have been able to say with Hugh of St. Victor: "He is yet delicate to whom his native land is sweet. But he is already strong to whom every soil is his country, and he is perfect to whom the whole world is a place of exile."[35] In fact, as in the *Divine Comedy* he feigns, also in the fateful year 1300 he suffered purgation on the Mount, and learned from a more spiritual teacher than Brunetto Latini how man truly eternizes himself in heaven.[36] And in the Earthly Paradise, symbol of right living on earth, Beatrice had also declared to him his true vocation of prophesying to men,—a declaration confirmed also by the shade of his ancestor Cacciaguida in Paradise.[37]

To wisdom through self-knowledge Dante came,[38] but

[34] *Hell*, i, 1–3.
[35] *Eruditio didascalia*, iii, 20.   Cited from E. G. Gardner, *Dante and the Mystics*, London, 1913, p. 150.
[36] Cf. *Hell*, xv, 82–85.   [37] *Purg.*, xxxiii; *Par.*, xvii.
[38] *Par.*, xxxiii, 143–5.

by "a way of sighs." It was true, as he said, that "the moving cause" of his odes to the Compassionate Lady was "not passion, but virtue"[39]—not his virtue indeed, but God's speaking in his heart; but he had obeyed the inspiration misunderstandingly—in life as in love; and so God had chastened him for his own good—by remorse for his disloyalty to Beatrice, by deprivation of the passing earthly glory for which he was in danger of sacrificing the everlasting glory. To himself he seemed to have lost forever Beatrice, and the heavenly blessedness also which her name signified. Blessedness is the state of heaven; blessedness lost is the state of hell. God's chastening then was as if to show Dante the hell to which his inordinate desire was leading him. "The fear of the Lord is the beginning of wisdom." So later will Beatrice say of her desperate expedient to save her disloyal lover:

> So low he fell that all expedients
>   For his salvation proved already short,
>   Except to show him those who have been lost.[40]

God's virtue will bring Dante to felicity at last—after being "made perfect in weakness."

Out of the logic of the New Life as "aided" by that of the Banquet thus springs the conception of the Comedy,[41] the term meaning for Dante a plain tale of reversal of fortune from bad to good.

[39] Banquet, I, ii, 122–3.
[40] Purg., xxx, 136–8.
[41] The epithet "Divine" was an addition of commentators.

III

THE DIVINE COMEDY

IN principle, the *Divine Comedy* is simply that part
of the personal confession of the *New Life* which comes
after Beatrice's death writ large. A subjective state is
magnified into one objective and universal. But recently
Jacopone da Todi had sung of "How the sinful soul is
hell, and then by the light of grace makes itself paradise." Perhaps it is mere coincidence, but Jacopone's
poem almost epitomizes the argument of the *Divine
Comedy*, and suggests transition from the subjective
treatment of the *New Life*. Such ideas were in the air.
Holy Scripture itself warranted them.[42] But for illustration of contemporary lyric treatment of the idea a
few lines from Jacopone may be roughly rendered.

> The soul that is sinful, likeness hath it of hell.
> House is it made of the Fiend; he hath claimed it for patri-
>   mony.
> Pride sitteth in it throned; it is worse than bedeviled.
> Shadows of envy enshroud it; for good it setteth a snare.
> There vestige of good is none, so is the mind beclouded.
> There fires of wrath are kindled that draw unto evil the
>   will.
> Turneth it about and goeth biting like any mad thing. . . .
>   *   *   *   *   *
> Come hither, people, and hear and marvel at that ye shall
>   see:
> The soul that was yesterday hell is today unto paradise
>   turned.
> From the Father is light descended; gift of His grace hath
>   He sent.
> Paradise so hath He made of the mind that was reprobate.
> Meekness hath He infused, and He hath broken pride,
> Which like a tempest the mind was bringing to ruin for-
>   ever.

[42] E. g., *II Sam.*, xxii; *Ps.*, xviii.

Pride hath He put to flight, and the heart hath enamored
  so
That to its neighbor it turns with embrace of charity. . . .
    *   *   *   *   *

O heart, be not ingrate, such good God hath given thee!
Live thou enamored forever of the life angelical![43]

The action of the *New Life* after Beatrice's death and
Dante's mourning develops rapidly by three episodes,—
that of the Compassionate Lady, that of the pilgrims,
and that of the final beatific vision.

The outcome of the episode of the Compassionate
Lady has already been stated. By perverse understanding
of Love's dictation—right in itself though equivocal for
Dante—he has renounced the heavenly for an earthly
desire. Brought to realization of guilt by an "overwhelming imagining" of his bliss, Beatrice, shame and misery
are his portion.[44] Through Beatrice he is indeed shown
in himself the lost folk.

Seeing the error of his ways and terrified by that hell
to which his error has been leading him, he would fain
retrace his steps. Divine mercy is prompt to guide. Certain persons, he says, had come from a far country to
Florence, drawn by the fame of the dead Beatrice. He
had been inspired to sing of their grief in finding her
no longer there. But the intention of his inspiration, as
he now sees, was deeper. These persons, he writes with
retrospective understanding, are like pilgrims to the
shrine of the *Veronica*, "that blessed image which Je-
sus Christ left us for ensample of His most glorious
countenance."[45] It is indeed right for them to comfort
themselves with that image, that "simulacrum," of the
true Desire of the World, and to strengthen their love

[43] *Laude di Frate Jacopone da Todi* . . . a cura di Giovanni
Ferri, Roma, 1910, p. 19.
[44] *New Life*, xl.   [45] *Ib.*, xli.

and faith by gazing on it. But foolish would it be, on the other hand, to worship the image for the reality— like the dog that, snatching at the shadow in the water below, dropped from his mouth the real bone.

Though the full import of this episode is not declared in the *New Life*, yet that his insight was already sufficiently cleared to perceive it dimly "as in a dream," Dante would indicate by his "rhymed words" next reported. In these he tells how his "pilgrim spirit" was uplifted by a "new intelligence" inspired by love to where Beatrice is in glory. There is his true country, his *patria*, to which as pilgrim he must return. Beatrice, he says, spoke to him; and her words seemed to be words of guidance and encouragement for his homing; but he was not yet able to grasp their transcendent meaning. His faith, however, has been made strong; and by that he shall regain, as St. Paul assures,[46] at last his true fatherland, the "city whose builder and maker is God," heavenly model of that earthly city made glorious by the divine image in Beatrice. Dante's present duty is therefore clear. He must "study" for enlightenment of his faith.

The first two of these three climactic episodes of the *New Life* constitute also the logical basis of the *Banquet*, though so overlaid by digressive argument as to lose their proper salience. Fittingly—as in a banquet of wisdom—the later-learned true meaning of the episodes is declared, and not—as in the *New Life*—actual misreading, or partial reading, for the nonce. Thus, as explained, the Compassionate Lady symbolizes the virtuous active life in due subordination to the religious life; and Dante's right relation to her is allegorically summed in his account of Marcia and her two husbands,

[46] *Hebrews*, xi. It would seem almost certain that Dante in writing this episode of the *New Life* had St. Paul's text in mind.

Cato and Hortensius.[47] At Cato's command, Marcia
married Hortensius that she might be fruitful; but, her
womanly task accomplished, she was fain in her old
age to return to Cato. So, says Dante, the Noble Soul
by God's command turns from contemplation of him
to fruitful activity, but, that fulfilled, would return again
to the blessedness of its contemplation. Dante himself
is the Noble Soul; Beatrice, his first love, represents
contemplation; the Compassionate Lady, action.

Supplemental to the parable of the pilgrims is that of
the angel at the tomb.[48] The three Marys—or the three
sects of the philosophy of the active life—vainly seek
Christ, the highest blessedness, in the tomb of this
world. There an angel—or "appetite of the soul" for wisdom—directs the seekers towards Galilee, where alone
on earth highest blessedness is to be found. For "Galilee"
means "whiteness," "a color more charged with material
light than any other," and so may properly signify contemplation, in which the spiritual Light of the World
is received. Dante's etymology may be quaint, but his
point is clear enough.[49]

The final episode of the New Life, the beatific vision,
is paralleled in the Banquet only by implication or brief
allusion; for, as Dante said, his book is one of temporal
and practical wisdom. He will not speak fully in it of the
"living Beatrice in glory,"—not, that is, of the supreme
blessedness of the vision of truth possessed by the elect
of God.

The opening scene of the Divine Comedy is, as has
been said above, the projection of Dante's moment of
spiritual peril upon an outer world of possible experience. That this world is informed and peopled by living

[47] Banquet, IV, xxviii, 97 ff.   [48] Ib., xxii, 134 ff.
[49] In Par., xxxi, 103–11, the parable of the pilgrims is again
developed to the same point.

symbols is for Dante no bar to its imaginative truth
to nature. To the mystic always, but to the thirteenth-
century mystic especially, nature is literally the hand-
writing of God, which those with spiritual insight may
decipher. So Hugh of St. Victor: "Contemplating what
God has done, we learn what is for us to do. All nature
speaks God. All nature teaches man."[50] For the poet-
mystic then allegory is true realism. The symbolic world
evoked by his imagination is in principle a true mirror
of the actual world created by God.

Astray in the dread forest of error, barred from the
height of rectitude by three bestial sins, Dante almost
despairs, when by grace of God through Beatrice, Virgil miraculously comes to his rescue. Yet since by Dante's
own fault the direct way to paradise is barred, he must
journey by a round-about, arduous, and sorrowful way
through hell and up the mount of purgatory. He is
indeed only repeating afresh in his own personal experience the penalty which Adam's fault imposed upon all.

To all men merciful guidance is given for return to
the lost Eden in conscience, the inner voice of reason
in moral issues. The sum of the dictates of that inner
voice of reason is moral philosophy. So moral philosophy
appears to Dante as incarnate in Virgil.

In thus apparently preferring Virgil before Aristotle
as his supreme guide of earthly conduct Dante is not
really inconsistent with his declaration of Aristotle's
philosophical supremacy. Aristotle is still in the *Divine
Comedy* "master of them that know,"[51] still Dante's
own master.[52] But in his *Aeneid*, Virgil, as Dante believed, applied in beauty Aristotle's wisdom to the moral
and political life of man. Moreover, Virgil was made
unwitting prophet of the coming of divine wisdom, the

---

[50] *Didascalia*, VI, v.   [51] *Hell*, iv, 131.
[52] *Par.*, viii, 120.

Word which was Christ, in his fourth eclogue. He
served, says Dante,

> like one, who walking in the night
> Carries a light behind, not for himself,
> But making wise those that do follow him.[53]

As persuasive interpreter of Aristotle's moral philosophy, and as the one of all pagans who in his inspiration
came nearest to the knowledge of Christ, Virgil was fit-
test guide to the threshold of the paradise purely earthly.
Politically, again, he prophesied that Roman Empire
actually foreordained to rule the temporal world. And
last, though not least, he had chastened his Aeneas in
the hell through which he was to lead Dante to his
salvation.[54]

Back to the lost Eden, the earthly paradise capping
the purgatorial mount, Virgil leads Dante. There in the
serene wood, gracious foil to the grim forest where Virgil had found him, appears Matilda. Singing, she goes
gathering flowers beside Lethe, the stream which washes
away guilty memories. To her Virgil commits further
guidance of his charge. He himself has led as far as in
his capacity lay. For to regain the Eden forfeited by
Adam was needful Christ's atonement, as later in paradise Beatrice will explain.[55] Only by humbling himself
as low as his first father, Adam, had in his folly presump-
tuously exalted himself on high, might man render just
satisfaction to offended God. And this of himself man
could not do, since self-humbling before God were
equally his duty though no sin had been committed.
Therefore to satisfy justice and mercy both, God took
the one way of humbling himself in vicarious sacrifice.
In this sacrifice for man of God as man, the moral

[53] Purg., xxii, 67–9.   [54] Aen., vi. Cf. Hell, ii, 10 ff.
[55] Par., vii.

law is at once fulfilled and transcended by divine love,
charity. In other words, through Christ a new moral law
was given to mankind for its guidance, not negativing
the old, but subordinating all the commandments to
one principle—love—with twofold application.[56] Fulfilment of this twofold law of love towards neighbor and
towards God is perfect living on earth as in heaven.

The place designed for perfect living on earth was
Eden:

> The root of mankind here was innocent.[57]

In readmitting Dante into Eden, therefore, Matilda sets
upon him that seal of innocence—rewon through Christ.
In other words, through her agency he is brought to realization of perfect living on earth as there might have
been for all mankind but for Eve's tempting.[58]

In so far, then, Matilda's service to him is just that
for which in the Banquet he had gratefully praised the
Compassionate Lady. Each revealed to him the moral
law in its application to this life, by fulfilment of which
earthly blessedness is won, Eden regained. Only, in the
Banquet a distinction is merely implied which in the
Divine Comedy is made explicit. In the teaching of Aristotle, as Dante in the Banquet had said, was embodied
virtually the moral law. But Aristotle as a man, even
like Dante himself, could only express his divinely inspired message, only note down the dictation of divine
love, in the measure of his human capacity of understanding. Those who came after might interpret the
record of Aristotle's message in his writings according
to their respective lights, even as Dante interpreted the
record of his own early poems. And to all Christians has
been given a great new light. So if Virgil interprets

---

[56] Cf. Matt., xxii, 36–40.   [57] Purg., xxviii, 142.
[58] Purg., xxix, 22–30.

Aristotle to Dante by the light of human reason in the
highest, Matilda reinterprets him in the new light of
divine revelation shed in Christ. In a word, she typifies
Christian-Aristotelianism, that "virtually Catholic opinion," which is in fact the philosophy hailed and expounded as the Compassionate Lady of *The Banquet*.

Thus Dante's "second love" of the *Banquet* is in the
Divine Comedy given a local habitation (in Eden) and
a name. But it must not hastily be inferred that the
gentle lady who from her window actually cast compassionate glances at the dejected lover,[59] would have responded to the name of Matilda. Such inference—which
has indeed been drawn—implies entire misunderstanding of Dante's symbolism. By her influence upon his life
at a critical moment, the lady of the window—whoever
she may have been—was the providential, though doubtless unconscious, means of bringing his life into accord
with the moral law. In function in so far equivalent to
the moral law, she may be taken as a symbol of that.
In the action of the *Divine Comedy* Matilda fulfils the
same function and is therefore identical with the Compassionate Lady as a symbol, but may well represent—
if anybody—another person. The law of Dante's symbolism is, so to speak, algebraic: equivalents may be
substituted for equivalents without changing the equa-
tion; but equivalence is not necessarily identity.

That behind the mask of Matilda was also a real personality who influenced Dante, and might in similar
fashion influence others, is suggested by the analogy of
his other characters. She should be no mere personified
abstraction, but a real symbol in the sense already explained. Possibly, Dante was glancing through her at
one or the other—or perhaps at both as one—of two
mystical nuns of the thirteenth century,—Mechthild of

[59] *New Life*, xxxvi.

Magdeburg and Mechthild of Hackedorn.[60]

While Dante rested on a rocky step just below the earthly paradise, he had fallen asleep and dreamed of a lady, young and fair, who went singing and gathering flowers to make her, she said, a garland. Her name was Leah.

> I deck me here to please me at my glass;
>   But from her mirror, where all day she sits,
>   My sister Rachel never turns away. . .
>   Seeing brings her content, as working me.[61]

This dream, which came to Dante as the star of love, Venus, was rising in the east, is manifest presage of his meeting with Matilda, the singing, flower-gathering lady of the earthly paradise. So by symbolic implication there presided over his meeting with Matilda the same angelic Intelligences of the third heaven as before had drawn his desire to the Compassionate Lady. And as the boon of the latter had been moral wisdom, "the virtue which maketh man blessed in his doing," so that moral wisdom is symbolized in the garland Matilda is weaving for herself of the flowers of good deeds. Presently, Dante will behold also Beatrice, counterpart of the Rachel of his dream, wearing the other garland of religious wisdom, symbol of devout contemplation.[62]

Thus is repeated in the *Divine Comedy* more clearly and graciously the interpretation of the relation between Dante's two loves, Beatrice and the Compassionate Lady, already indicated in the *Banquet* by the allegorized story of the sisters Mary and Martha, in which, according to Dante, Mary's "part"—the contemplative life—is declared to be "best," though Martha's "part"—

[60] Cf. E. G. Gardner: *Dante and the Mystics*, London, 1913, viii.

[61] Purg., xxvii, 103–5, 108.   [62] Purg., xxx, 31, 68.

the active life—is also "good."[63] Matilda—or the Compassionate Lady rightly followed—and Beatrice together reveal to him the "science of love," Christian wisdom,—the one in the moral aspect, the other in the religious. This symbolism, moreover, exactly agrees with that of one whom Dante sees in paradise and calls "in speculation more than human,"—the great mystic, Richard of St. Victor.[64] In his work *On the preparation of the mind for contemplation*, Richard explains symbolically the Old Testament characters Rachel and Leah—prophetic types of Mary and Martha—in a way peculiar to himself.[65] Leah—and therefore her Dantesque ectype Matilda—symbolizes "affection inflamed by divine inspiration, composing itself to the norm of justice." Her boon is accordingly perfection of the active life, the felicity of *doing* God's will. Rachel—and therefore her Dantesque ectype Beatrice—symbolizes "reason exalting itself to the contemplation of heavenly wisdom." And her boon is accordingly perfection of the contemplative life, the felicity of *knowing* God—so far as man on earth may know him.

Thus together Matilda and Beatrice fulfil in symbol the Christian life,—merit of good deeds supplemented by grace of communion with God together preparing the soul for salvation, for the

> glory that shall be, which is produced
> By grace divine and merit that precedes.[66]

For governance of the Christian life there exist by divine institution Church and Empire. They as militant powers would establish on earth again the innocence and peace of Eden. Appropriately then in the earthly para-

[63] *Banquet*, IV, xvii, 85 ff.   [64] *Par.*, x, 131–2.
[65] Cf. Gardner, *op. cit.*, pp. 271–2.
[66] *Par.*, xxv, 68–9.

dise Matilda leads Dante to where he beholds the Church Militant advancing in symbolic procession to meet him. And later, after absolving him, Beatrice interprets prophetically the transformations of the Chariot and the Tree, symbols of Church and Empire, and bids him declare his vision and her prophecy to men. She then recommits him to Matilda, who immerses him in the waters of Eunoe,—or in other words reconsigns him to the active life which shall give consciousness of merit. He shall see his earthly task clear, and the reward of its fulfilment.

> I came up out of the most holy wave
>   Made over in such wise as are new trees
>   That do renew themselves with foliage new,
> Pure and disposed to mount unto the stars.[67]

The insistence here on his *new* life won through his two loves—Matilda representing the Compassionate Lady given duly subordinate allegiance—would seem to bind the climax of the *Purgatory* with that of the *New Life*.

Before this new life in promise of felicity through right doing, was needed absolution of past sin. In Dante's symbolic language, Eunoe is without virtue unless Lethe also be tasted.[68] Need of absolution is of course universal, for no son of Adam can be without sin. In so far, Dante may represent Everyman; his experience is typical; but his confession of sin is also personal. Indeed nowhere else in the whole poem does he approach so near to the intimate tone of St. Augustine's *Confessions*; and it is upon this occasion alone that he—dramatically through the accusing Beatrice—names himself.[69]

[67] *Purg.*, xxxiii, 143–5. The translation is mine. Johnson hardly brings out the symbolic side of the repetition—*novelle—rinnovellate—novella*.
[68] *Purg.*, xxviii, 127–32.   [69] *Ib.*, xxx, 55.

48 Dante

The situation is dramatically identical with that in
the New Life where the apparition of Beatrice rebukes
Dante for unfaithfulness in giving his heart to the Compassionate Lady.[70] Indeed Beatrice explicitly associates
the transgression for which she now rebukes her lover,
with the time immediately following her death:

> Upon the threshold of my second age
>> As soon as I was standing, and changed life,
>> He gave himself to others, leaving me.[71]

Allegorically, as already explained, Dante surrendered
himself to the Compassionate Lady, to the active life—
not properly, as a means of advancing the glory of God,
but as an end. Having lost touch with truth, he fell
victim to illusion.

> The present things
> With their false pleasure turned my steps away,
> Soon as your face was hidden from my sight.[72]

So far the confession of the New Life is virtually reit-
erated. But Beatrice's retort would imply that her present rebuke was not for Dante's transgression with the
Compassionate Lady, but for a repetition of the offence
in kind:

> E'en two or three the young bird will await,
>> But in the sight of those full-fledged, in vain
>> Is the net spread, and is the arrow shot.[73]

Not only in naturally "fervid and passionate" youth had
Dante offended, but also again in his mature age, properly "temperate and virile."[74] By a single word Bea-

[70] New Life, xl.
[71] Purg., xxx, 124–6. Dante's text "diessi altrui" may also
mean—"He gave him to another."
[72] Purg., xxxi, 34–6.   [73] Ib., xxxi, 61–3.
[74] Banquet, I, i, 116–8.

trice suggests the nature of the offence: there should
not have weighted down his wings

> a damsel young,
> Or other vanity of so brief use.[75]

To a young damsel, or *pargoletta*, Dante addressed
several odes and a sonnet or two. For her stony-hearted-
ness he called her a "stone" (*pietra*), and declared that
she, Medusa-like, turned also his heart to stone,[76] and
again that for her he had "howled as in a hot caldron."[77]

To no one else did Dante make such passionate love.
Nowhere else is his appeal so frankly, even brutally
sensuous. If the odes to the stony-hearted Damsel were
allegorical—as the proposed inclusion of them in the
Banquet might be taken to imply,—at least their dramatic art is worthy of Shakspere. There is evidence, however, that they concern a real passion. In purgatory the
poet Bonagiunta murmurs the name "Gentucca," and
foretells—from the standpoint of the ideal date of the
poem, 1300—a damsel who shall endear to Dante Bonagiunta's native Lucca, whatever scandal ensue.[78] Dante
appears to have been in Lucca during the summer of
1314. An early commentary on the *Divine Comedy* identifies "Gentucca" as Gentucca Morla, wife of a certain
Cosciorino Fondora.[79]

In the moral dialectic of the *Divine Comedy*, Gentucca—as for convenience we may call the stony-hearted
Damsel[80]—repeats for Dante the rôle of the Compassionate Lady. But with Gentucca he repeats with em-

[75] *Purg.*, xxxi, 59–60.
[76] "*Amor tu vedi ben che questa donna,*" l. 18.
[77] "*Così nel mio parlar voglio esser aspro,*" l. 60.
[78] *Purg.*, xxiv, 37, 43–5.
[79] Cf. Paget Toynbee, *Dante Alighieri*, London, 1910, p. 97.
[80] The identification of the two is of course only plausible,
but is not important in the present connection.

phasis the error confessed in the *New Life* and explained in the *Banquet*. Only Matilda's was the just consolation allowed by divine love. Hers was a comforting towards Beatrice, not away from her.

Thus is finally verified Dante's enigmatic statement in the *Banquet* that the "moving cause" of his seeming-passionate odes was yet "not passion but virtue." In the divine impulse moving him to love the Compassionate Lady there was for him delphic ambiguity. By one interpretation passion indeed spoke,—such inordinate desire as blindly bound him to the "lady of the window" in his youth, and again to the stony-hearted Gentucca in his manhood. But such disloyal passion was not the true intention of Love. That divine intention is made clear allegorically in the *Banquet*, dramatically in the *Comedy*. Matilda is gracious to him not that she may wean him from Beatrice, but to prepare him for reunion with her.

Dante in his blindness had seemed to thwart Love's beneficent purpose; but Love's "strength is made perfect in weakness." Gentucca, he said, turned his heart to stone. He "boiled for her in the hot caldron." By these passionate metaphors he had thought to express the thwarting of his evil desires; but looking backward, he can now reread them as oracular dictations of a higher inspiration. Under the spell of the Siren[81] he had become at once hardened of heart and burning in the lusts of the flesh. In his own words unconsciously he had prophesied the hell which gaped before him. By the grace of God in reminder of Beatrice he had been afraid and ashamed. So in his dream of the Siren, it was a holy woman who had disclosed for him the secret horror of the temptress.[82] And now after due penance, he is given remission of sin. Matilda, right blessedness

[81] *Purg.*, xxxi, 45; xix, 1–60. [82] *Ib.*, xix, 26 ff.

of this life, dips him in the merciful oblivion of Lethe. And so the shadow passes of her that was stony-hearted and had turned his heart and head to stone.[83] The "vanity of so brief use," which is earthly desire, no longer even exists for him.[84] Then Matilda confers her boon of Eunoe—consciousness of merit—by which, grace added, he shall at last regain "salvation," the lost *salute* of Beatrice.

By him, as Beatrice declares, merit is to be won in the active life. Therein lies his God-given capacity. The injunction of the Intelligences of Venus as explained in the *Banquet*, is in the *Divine Comedy* dramatically repeated by Beatrice. His unfaithfulness forgiven, he would fain indulge his "ten year thirst" of her loveliness. But her handmaidens, the Seven Virtues, forbid. "Too absorbed," they cry, and turn away his eyes from her.[85] Presently, Beatrice herself explains the symbolic prohibition:

A forest-dweller here a little while,
   Thou shalt with me for aye be citizen
   Of that Rome, where a Roman too is Christ.
To profit then the world of evil life
   Fix now thine eyes upon the car, and when
   Thou hast returned, write down what thou hast seen.[86]

She comforts and directs him as Christ comforted and directed the Apostles. Indeed, to his deputed guides and comforters on earth, the Virtues, she uses the very words of Christ, according to the *Vulgate*:

[83] *Ib.*, xxxiii, 73–5.
[84] *Ib.*, xxxiii, 91–3.
[85] *Purg.*, xxxii, 1–9. Later, in the heaven of the Sun, the situation is in symbolic effect repeated: Dante absorbed in contemplation of God, is recalled to consider the teachers and preachers of God, his destined masters. *Par.*, x, 58 ff.
[86] *Purg.*, xxxii, 100–5.

> Modicum, et non videbitis me,
> Et iterum, beloved sisters mine,
> Modicum, et vos videbitis me.[87]

Dante meekly acquiesces:

> My Lady, all my need
> You know, and what is good for it.[88]

So Beatrice instructs him according to his need, even
as the white-raimented youth of the New Life had in-
structed him according to his need—then.[89] And it is
the "good part"—Martha's part—of the active worker
that Beatrice lays down for him. Love dictates; it is
for him to bring the message to men.

> Do thou take note; and, as I utter them,
> See that thou mark these words for those who live
> The life that is a running unto death.[90]

Perfect clarity of insight indeed he has not yet. Sin,
though forgiven, has left its benumbing trace. "Stone"
she was who had been his unholy desire, stony she has
left his mind. Yet though incapable of transmitting Beatrice's intellectual light unchanged, he may at least con-
vey her intention as by a symbol appealing to sense.
So Beatrice:

> But, as I see thee in thine intellect
> Made as of stone, and, stony, darkened so,
> The light of what I say is dazzling thee,
> I also will that thou shouldst bear it hence,
> If not in words, yet painted in thy mind,
> Even as pilgrims bring the palm-wreathed staff.[91]

In the measure of his still clouded understanding, then,
Dante's task will be to declare true doctrine of man's
civil life under a Church restored to her pristine purity

[87] Ib., xxxiii, 10–2; cf. John, xvi, 16.
[88] Purg., xxxiii, 29–30.   [89] New Life, xii, 40–1.
[90] Purg., xxxiii, 52–4.   [91] Ib., xxxiii, 73–8.

and an Empire pacified in itself and pacifier of a distraught earth. For such is Beatrice's meaning under the images recorded by Dante. From political activity itself Dante had been withdrawn by the will of God providentially manifest in his exile. His is the task of teacher and prophet of true policy,—which is also service and fulfilling of the active life.

The true policy he will declare is in effect that which the angels announcing Christ had declared—"On earth peace to men of good will."[92] In their declaration is implied the gospel of him whom they announced, and that gospel is the law of heaven. Therefore, as to recall Dante from sin Beatrice had shown him the state of the lost folk in hell, so now for his encouragement in goodness and to enable him better to convert others to goodness, she will show him the state of the blest folk in the many mansions of God's house.

These mansions are nothing other than sign and symbol of the heavenly law itself, which is charity or holy love.[93] As Dante rises through them, realizing more and more perfectly that law of love, the "stoniness" of his intellect softens, the light of Beatrice no longer perplexes and dazzles; until in very truth more than humanly he knows God, and so knowing, more than humanly loves him. On the way, love and knowledge mutually increase each other; in the end, knowledge and love are one.

The final climax of the *Divine Comedy* is the mystic vision of the Trinity. For a rapt instant Dante's thought penetrated the divine essence itself, and

> saw within its depths enclosed all that,
> Which in the universe is scattered leaves,
> With love as in a single volume bound.[94]

[92] Cf. On Monarchy, I, iv.
[93] Cf. G. Busnelli: *Il concetto e l'ordine del "Paradiso" dantesco*, 2 vols., Città di Castello, 1911–2. Cf. also *infra*, chap. ii.
[94] Par., xxxiii, 85–7.

Again the question recurs, was this experience also actual? Did Dante, like St. Paul, St. Francis of Assisi, St. Catherine of Sienna,—like his nearer master, St. Thomas Aquinas,—claim for himself the mystic ecstasy in which the spirit is miraculously brought face to face with God, and yet returns again to the earthly body? Did he really visit the heavenly Beatrice,—meaning heavenly blessedness itself?

Certainly, self-conviction of such experience would supremely justify his offering himself for example to others. And in his epistle to Can Grande della Scala sent with his *Paradise* and explanatory of it, he certainly seems to write of his mystic vision not as of a poetic phantasy but as of a solemn fact, a miracle vouchsafed to him, sinner though he was.[95] As Dante was writing to his patron not in the character of his dramatic protagonist, but in his own person, the tone of the passage in question would seem defensible only if sincere. And after all, there is no inherent reason why Dante should not have had as full and intimate conviction of this culminating religious experience as any other person. Habituated to the thought of him as man of the world, artist, philosopher, we may feel the added title of "saint" strange,—but is there any good reason for denying him it?

For this *momentum intelligentiae*, this instant intuition of the divine essence, the human intellect as such is incompetent. The human intellect works upon sense-data. It is discursive, not intuitive. To reach it, therefore, divine revelation must translate itself into the forms of sense-knowledge.[96] And such condescension of divine love is expressed for Dante in Beatrice. It is therefore fitting that his intuitive moment, in which his intellect

[95] *Epis.*, x, par. 28. Cf. Gardner, *Dante and the Mystics*, I, iii; also Udny, *Dante's Mysticism*, *Contemp. Rev.*, April, 1914.
[96] *Par.*, iv, 40–9.

miraculously transcends its human limitations and is cleared from "all clouds of his mortality" should be attained through a higher influence in principle than even Beatrice. As Virgil—pagan philosophy of the unillumined reason—gives place to Matilda—Christian philosophy of the illumined reason, so Beatrice—dogmatic theology of the discursive and illumined reason—gives place to St. Bernard—mystic theology of the intuitive and illumined reason. The organon of mystic theology is the higher logic of love; and in his epistle to Can Grande Dante cites three authorities in this "science of love,"— Richard of St. Victor in his book de Contemplatione, Bernard in his de Consideratione, and Augustine in his de Quantitate Animae. Of the three Bernard is chosen for having, through devoted service of the Virgin Mary, supremely attained the "intellect of love" by which the beatific vision is won.[97]

Reviewing the course of Dante's personal confession as made progressively in the New Life, the Banquet, and the Divine Comedy, we come now to understand his method and its justification. Inspired as one "in a dream," he had early in the New Life outlined the stages of his redemption, so offering on the sure testimony of first-hand experience example of the merciful providence of God. Already in that first work was declared the agency through which divine love manifested itself to him in the increasing measure of his spiritual capacity. Beatrice was that agency while she lived on earth. After her translation, her influence was in the design of providence to be vicariously exerted by the Compassionate Lady, likeness and reminder of her—as she was for him likeness and reminder of the divine Being. The Compassionate Lady was sent to him as the Holy Spirit descended upon the Apostles after Christ had left them.

[97] Par., xxxi, 100–2, 109–11.

If Dante in his human blindness awhile mistook that consolation in this life for the consolation of this life, yet in time his eyes were mercifully opened.

As the *New Life* obscurely intimates,[98] the right influence of the Compassionate Lady came from her paler likeness to Beatrice, as the "Veronica" draws mankind to him whose likeness it is. At bottom Dante's one true comforter, one truly "compassionate lady," is Beatrice,[99] the eternal "blessedness" her name signifies is for all men the one ultimate consolation in life and for life.

Indeed, Dante's life-pilgrimage was but a quest for the right "compassionate lady." Various others he mistook for her in his blindness; and since love is like calling to like, his loves were mirrors of his own mind. To him stony-minded with sinful passion conformed "Gentucca," the "stony-one," *la Pietra,*—a love indeed not of comfort but despair. To him softened by penitence and illumined by grace conformed the radiant Matilda, spirit of earthly perfection. But when he became spiritually raised above earth, "transhumanized," he sought the more than earthly perfection of Beatrice, of whom Matilda was but a paler likeness. And finally, when he had transcended all the nine heavens and stood in the very presence of God, he amorously sought that mediating glory of which the glory of Beatrice herself was but a paler reflection,—the glory of the Virgin Mother, *donna pietosa* in very deed of all mankind.[100]

In this process there is reminder of a quaint image by Dante's friend Guido Cavalcanti in one of his poems:

> Something befalleth me when she is by
>   Which unto reason can I not make clear:
>   Meseems I see forth through her lips appear
>   Lady of fairness such that faculty
>   Man hath not to conceive; and presently

[98] xxxvii, 1–6.   [99] *Cf. Hell,* ii, 133.
[100] *Par.,* xxxiii, 1–21.

> Of this one springs another of new grace,
> Who to a star then seemeth to give place,
> Which saith: "Lo, thy salvation is with thee."[101]

From the sensible beauty buds, as it were, the spiritual; from the spiritual, the ideal; from the ideal, the divine, which flowers in heaven and is the lover's "salvation" [salute].

Beatrice's words to Virgil quoted by him to encourage the hesitating Dante show the process reversed.[102] Our Lady, divinely compassionate, moves St. Lucy—apparently Dante's patron-saint—to move Beatrice, his love, to move Virgil to lead Dante to salvation. Or, allegorically, divine mercy (the Virgin) sends its illuminating grace (Lucy) to light Dante's reason (Virgil) back to the principles of right living and true believing as defined by Christian moral philosophy (Matilda) and theology (Beatrice).

In impersonal edification the Divine Comedy caps the two earlier works, revealing the "new life" beyond the grave in imaginative truth, and offering a "banquet" of wisdom for this life. Dante has seen all truth in God. Although he may not be able to write out clear the ineffable vision, he will express under such images as remain painted in his mind what it is expedient for his fellowmen to know.[103] So doing, he will indeed praise God by imitating him; for the universe itself is but a vaster image under which God expresses to men the wisdom which, listened to, redeems. The universe is the Word of God made legible; theology—science of the Word—is therefore the science of sciences, key to all wisdom. Any consideration of Dante's impersonal teaching must accordingly begin with his theology. Theological conclusions are for him major premises to all others, whether in moral, natural, or political science.

---

101 Ballata, Veggio ne gli occhi.
102 Hell, ii, 94 ff.   103 Cf. Purg., xxxiii, 73–8.

CHAPTER II

THE TEACHING OF DANTE

CHAPTER II

The Teaching of Dante

"All nature speaks God. All nature teaches man."
Hugh of St. Victor.

SYMBOLICALLY shadowed forth through the personal confession of the *New Life* is the gospel of human redemption through the love of Christ and for Christ. The "way of sighs" by which the glorified Beatrice draws Dante to herself is spiritually identical with the way of salvation in Christ. The cardinal act of divine justice and mercy in the Atonement is in principle reënacted in the death of Beatrice. In the Compassionate Lady, as Dante at first perversely conceived her consolation, is symbolized the Tempter, offering "the kingdoms of the world" in exchange for the kingdom of heaven. In yielding to the temptation Dante repeated the sin of

Adam. In visiting him in her mortal form to save him
from his sin,[1] Beatrice played again the rôle of the Re-
deemer condescending to take on manhood to save men.

The New Life is built up, as I believe, upon such subtle symbolic correspondences. So far from being an
ingenuous diary of the heart, it is an almost uniquely
complex piece of literary goldsmith's art. The subtlety,
however, is in the design. The philosophy of life presented in the New Life is no more than Christian com-
monplace. In the Banquet, indeed, Dante professes his
ignorance of philosophy up to the time of Beatrice's
death; and doubtless in comparison with the profound
theologian of the Divine Comedy the poet of the New
Life was inexpert. But it is possible to take Dante's retrospective self-depreciation too literally. The expert is
likely to be scornful of his novitiate. Also, it is frequently overlooked that the disclaimer is made not for
the composer of the book, but for the hero of it—or
rather of the first two-thirds of it,—who was several
years younger. Moreover, Dante is dramatically concerned to make the least of his then knowledge. Wishing
to identify wisdom presently gained of philosophy with
the consolation of the Compassionate Lady, he naturally represents the conquest of his mind by philosophy to have been as sudden and overwhelming as the
conquest of his heart by her. He paints himself as one
upon whose intellectual darkness has been thrown a great
light. The New Life itself, on the other hand, is dedicated to the young Dante's "first friend," Guido Cavalcanti, in contemporary opinion one of the most notable
philosophers of the age. In the book Dante acknowledges as his master the "sage" Guido Guinicelli, also
a notable philosopher. Now that Dante at nearly thirty
was quite obtuse to the precise intellectual interests both

[1] New Life, xl, 4–8.

of his "first friend" and intellectual intimate[2] and of his acknowledged and admired master is incredible. At the same time, it may well be that in the first enforced and bitter idleness of exile Dante sank himself with new intensity in rigorous study.

The *Banquet*, as its title implies, was designed even more to distribute the wisdom acquired by its author than to vindicate his love-poetry. Even the vindication itself, in explaining the odes as philosophical allegories, becomes a carrier of impersonal teaching. And a huge amount of miscellaneous information is obtruded by the way. Besides its subtle justification of the "second love," the *Banquet* is chiefly valuable as a kind of prosaic footnote to the *Divine Comedy*. For in it, Dante's thought, not transfigured into poetry, is at times more easily caught up with.

THE TEACHING OF THE DIVINE COMEDY

The *Divine Comedy* is virtually an epitome of theology, or *summa theologiae*, dramatized and set. Christian theology is the system of thought built up by the Church through her "fathers" and doctors on the revelations of Scripture.[3] According to Scripture two laws have been revealed to men,—by Moses the law of retribution, by Christ the law of love. Christ has not abrogated the Mosaic law, but once for all in the Atonement satisfied it for those who through faith are made one with him. For such, however, as know not or reject Christ, only the law of retribution—"eye for eye, tooth for tooth,"[4] holds. So the law that governs the punishments of hell is altogether retributory. Dante makes Bertran de Born, who

[2] Cf. Cavalcanti's famous sonnet to Dante, *infra*, p. 197.
[3] So in the heaven of the Sun Dante makes the circles of the Church fathers and doctors revolve about Beatrice as "revelation." *Par.*, x, 64–6.   [4] *Exod.*, xxi, 23 *et seq.*

goes carrying his severed head like a lantern, explain for instance:

> Father and son I set at mutual war. . .
> As I divided those who were thus joined,
>   My own brain I am carrying, alas!
>   Divided from its source within this trunk.
> Thus retribution is observed in me.[5]

In paradise, on the other hand, the one law is of love. "O Love that governest the heavens," cries Dante.[6] And Piccarda in paradise argues from charity, love of God, as the basic law of the blest.[7]

Although it is natural to speak of Dante's three kingdoms of the otherworld, the implication is not altogether accurate. Purgatory is really rather a temporal colony of heaven than an independent and parallel third kingdom. Those who sojourn in it have won their citizenship in heaven, for all that they are for a while in detention. To call them "prisoners of hope"[8] is misleading in so far as the idea of "hope" seems to contain that of possible disappointment; whereas for all who have passed the portal of purgatory, salvation is certain. Temptation is put behind them forever.[9] Their sole motive is charity, love of the supreme good.[10] Only, inasmuch as in their mortal lives there had been mixed in with this holy love other loves, perverted or defective or excessive,[11] in order to attain the perfect peace they must atone for these disordered loves. Satisfaction for sin prevented by death is still demanded by divine justice; but the penance is not, properly speaking, exacted; the penitent yearns to it as a lover to make himself

---

[5] *Hell*, xxviii, 136, 139–42.   [6] *Par.*, i, 74.
[7] "S'essere in carità è qui *necesse*." *Par.*, iii, 77.
[8] The title of a book on Dante's *Purgatory*.
[9] *Purg.*, xi, 19–24.   [10] *Ib.*, xvii, 85.
[11] *Ib.*, xvii, 19–139.

more beautiful in the eyes of his beloved.[12] Through welcome torments the shades go

> Purging away the cloudiness of earth,

asking also human prayers

> to help them wash away
> The marks that they bore hence, that they may rise,
> Made clean and light, up to the wheeling stars.[13]

In the last words of the *Paradise* Dante returns to the keynote of his moral scale:

> To the high fantasy here power failed;
>   But now was turning my desire and will,
>   Like to a wheel that evenly is moved,
> The Love that moves the sun and the other stars.

"Desire" and "will," subdued to charity, are so made perfectly harmonious with each other. The prayer of the Christian suppliant has been heard: "O God, who makest the minds of the faithful to be of one *will*; grant unto thy people to love what thou commandest, and to *desire* what thou dost promise; that amidst the various changes of the world our hearts may there be fixed where true joys abide."[14] The naturally good will of humanity, alienated from good by Adam's sin, was restored by the Atonement; but human desire may yet be led astray by the Siren of *seeming good*.[15] This is the potential tragedy of the Christian life on earth. In purgatory there is division still between will and desire, but not a tragic division. The penitent's will is to be with God; but his desire is first to purge that which had been in the earthly

[12] *Purg.*, xvi, 31–2. *Cf.* ii, 75.   [13] *Ib.*, xi, 30, 34–6.
[14] Collect of Fourth Sunday after Easter, Sacramentary of Gelasius.
[15] *Purg.*, xix. *Cf. Par.*, v, 7–12.

life sinful desire.[16] He would give satisfaction for past
sin by present pain. So in purgatory as in hell the *lex
talionis*, the law of retribution, prevails,—only in purgatory love transforms punishment into glad piety.

DIRECT TEACHING IN THE DIVINE COMEDY

As the avowed purpose of the *Divine Comedy* is in-
culcation of knowledge which is moral power,[17] Dante
is not content to present merely the dramatic pilgrim-
age of a soul from earth through hell and purgatory to
heaven. He steps out of the dramatic frame to comment
and explain, or to pass judgment. Dialogue is naturally,
however, his main form of direct teaching. Like all else
in the delicate economy of the poem, the dialogue is
subtly adjusted to the local situation. The pilgrim's own
mind is subdued to his temporary environment. In hell,
where is lost "the good of the intellect," not only are
the names of Christ or Beatrice not mentioned, but between Dante and Virgil or the various shades met with
there is—with one exception—no high speculative discourse. The one exception is Virgil's lecture on the moral
topography of hell. Dante listens docilely—like a school-
boy, without much inquisitiveness. His mind is bent on
personities and matters-of-fact. In all literalness, the
sermon of the *Hell* is by "horrible examples." Not until
well within the gate of purgatory does Dante raise a serious question of doctrine;[18] and to the last in purgatory
his mind is still "stony."[19] Virgil, too, conscious of his
lack of the higher insight of revelation and grace, is ten-
tative in his explanations, ever referring Dante to Bea-

---

[16] *Ib.*, xxi, 64–6.
[17] *Cf.* Epistle to Can Grande, par. 15–6.
[18] *Purg.*, xv, 40 ff. A minor doubt is raised and resolved in
Purg., vi, 28–48.
[19] *Ib.*, xxxiii, 73–4.

trice to come.[20] When Beatrice does come—in the earthly paradise,—her tone is at once one of authority, but she must still use the figurative or picture-language suited to Dante's sense-veiled understanding.[21] It is expedient for him now to see, but still as through a glass darkly.

The issues raised in purgatory concern moral responsibility in practical human living, whether personal or of church and state. Love is analyzed as the great dynamic force in life, instinctive in itself, yet in its objects subject to the inhibitions of reason, and so a moral agency. Behind the moral individual, protecting and guiding him, are state and church, embodiments of the law and the gospel,—though unhappily at odds for the time being with each other.[22]

In paradise, as he ascends sphere beyond sphere to the tenth heaven of that "light intellectual" in which the Creator himself becomes visible to the creature,[23] Dante's own intellectual vision grows keener and keener. In proportion, Beatrice can disclose to him more and more of her glory without dazzlement,[24] until at last he is able to see her as she is, unveiled.[25] His vision is indeed still of mortal kind; the gate of his understanding is still sense.[26] Later he reaches beyond even Beatrice, beyond truth humanly comprehensible. At the prayer of St. Bernard to the Virgin, that higher "lady of pity" by her intercession disperses for him "all clouds of his mortality";[27] his insight becomes intuitive of things-in-themselves.

Deep in proportion to Dante's progressively deepening insight are the conversations in paradise. His ques-

20 E. g., Purg., vi, 46–8; xv, 76–8; xviii, 46–8.
21 Ib., xxxiii, 73–8. Cf. Par., iv, 40–8.
22 Purg., xvi, 82 ff.; xxxii–xxxiii.
23 Par., xxx, 100–2.   24 Ib., v, 1–9.
25 Ib., xxiii, 46–8.   26 Ib., xxi, 61.
27 Ib., xxxiii, 31–3; 52–7.

tionings search closer and closer to the heart of things.[28]
Indeed, taken as a whole the conversations between
Dante and Beatrice round the great circle of Christian
cosmology. In the three lower heavens, over which earth
casts its shadow, Beatrice builds up from the leads of
her disciple the doctrine of the derivation of the Many
from the One, explicating so the opening tercet and text
of the canticle:

> The glory of the One who moves all things
> Penetrates through the universe, resplendent
> In one part more and in another less.

The first nine cantos establish theologically the premises on which Dante in his essay on *Monarchy* bases his
theory of the worldstate. God's temporal object is the
perfecting of mankind to fill up the vacant ranks of the
rebel angels.[29] Man's potentialities cannot be realized
in a void; only by social reactions may the individual
attain his full spiritual stature. Society, like all organ-
isms, necessarily involves diversity of function.[30] Diversity of function implies diversity of gift and power; and
to produce such diversity among men is the principal
final cause of the diversity of the stars, of the spotted
moon.[31] Incidentally, representatives of each of these
lower heavens—Piccarda, Justinian, Charles Martel—em-
phasize for Dante's benefit the duty of contentment in
one's appointed lot of service on earth as in heaven.[32]

Dante sharply divides from the rest these nine cantos
dealing with the three lower and earth-related heavens.
In the tenth canto, before telling of ascent into the
Sun, he makes a fresh start, invoking the reader to real-

---

[28] By such questioning all knowledge grows. *Par.*, iv, 124 ff.
[29] Cf. *Banquet* II, vi, 95–9.
[30] *Par.*, viii, 115 ff.   [31] *Par.*, ii.
[32] *Ib.*, iii, 64 ff.; vi, 118–26; viii, 91 ff.

ize how "the exalted wheels" of the heavens, hitherto stressed as agencies of diversity, also in their harmonious operation reveal the unity of God above and behind them, and so draw the Many back to the One. The first two tercets of the canto give the new text:

> Looking upon His own Son with the Love
> Which is eternally breathed forth by both,
> The Power primal and ineffable
> Made with such order whatsoe'er revolves
> Through mind or space, that he who looks on it
> Can not remain without a taste of Him.

These two texts, set at the beginning respectively of the first and tenth cantos, on the relations of the Many and the One, supreme metaphysical issue, are the two summarizing theses of the doctrine reported in the Paradise. As usual, Dante reinforces logical by visible prominence: no other canto in the canticle opens with a doctrinal thesis.

In respect to the second thesis—the return of the Many to the One, or reconciliation of man with God—Dante's instruction runs parallel to his ascent through the heavens. In the three lowest heavens—those of "blame"[33]— the Atonement is explained to him with all its sanctions and implications.[34] Beatrice is by right his teacher, but Justinian's averment and illustration of the divine right of the Roman Empire form a premiss to her argument.[35] For if the Crucifixion had not been sanctioned by Pilate as imperial representative of the divinely constituted authority over men, it would have been only a crime of the Jews alone, and not also, as God intended, a vicarious sacrifice accepted by all mankind.

By the Atonement, however, man was not advanced

[33] Par., iv, 58–60.   [34] Ib., vii.
[35] Ib., vi.

in perfection beyond his earthly beginning, but merely brought back to that, and enabled to make a fresh start.[36] In the higher heavens—those of "honor"—Dante learns, as well as symbolically experiences, the ways open for man's positive advancement towards the perfect life; and the instruction is dramatically summed in Dante's examination before the Apostles Peter, James, and John on the three theological virtues—or virtues which lead from earthly to heavenly perfection—of faith, hope, and charity.[37] Bitterest denunciation is constant, on the other hand, of wilful and wayward mankind, that even in the high places of church and empire is ever turning its back on these clearly defined ways of salvation. The degenerate world is in its "last age"[38] of rapid dissolution; the roll of the saved is almost called; few thrones in heaven remain to be filled.[39]

Topics of conversation are carefully related to the localities in which the conversations are held. Thus, in paradise, for instance, the chief conclusion reached in the Moon, sphere of *mutability*, is of the sovereign power of the will to remain *constant* against attempted compulsion. In the meekly self-effacing planet Mercury—

Veiled unto mortals with another's rays,—[40]

after rehearsal of the legitimate world-glory of the Roman Eagle, there is discussed the vainglory of the first man, Adam, that necessarily called for the self-humbling of the "new man," Christ. In amorous Venus,—now turned Sunward, now away,[41] as human love is turned now to light, now to darkness,—the question is of begetting, and how the stars may break the line of family likeness which mere carnal reproduction would make

[36] *Ib.*, vii, 145–8.   [37] *Par.*, xxiv–xxvi.
[38] *Banquet*, II, xv, 115–6.   [39] *Par.*, xxx, 131–2.
[40] *Ib.*, v, 129.   [41] *Par.*, viii, 12.

absolute. In the radiant Sun, from the question whether the blest spirits shall be always radiant springs declaration of the resurrection of the glorified body. In fiery Mars Dante's courage is tested by Cacciaguida's prophecy of ill. In equable Jupiter divine justice is asserted, even against human understanding,—as in the case of damnation of "invincible ignorance." In Saturn, sphere of the contemplatives, is broached the mystery of predestination, intelligible not even to the Seraphim, who of all contemplate God most nearly,—so immeasurably beyond the capacity of his creatures are the designs of God. In the stellar heaven, where is figured the triumph of the human elect, are discussed the triumph-giving virtues of faith, hope and charity. In the *Primum Mobile*, or first mover of things, rises the problem of creation. In the Empyrean, or quiet heaven, there is no questioning; for with the final beatific vision comes intuition of all truth, and so stilling of every desire of the mind.[42]

The Lesson of the Symbolism of the Three Kingdoms

This teaching by dramatic dialogue is but small part of the teaching of the *Divine Comedy*. The three kingdoms themselves of the other world in their structure and topography, their climates and landscapes, their inhabitants—human or animal or monstrous—are definite symbols, picture-language, of moral and religious truth.

So to present a world which is also a natural allegory is for Dante no mere arbitrary device of a didactic poet. For him the real world itself is just such a natural allegory. To every one who holds communion with her, Nature speaks not only a various but also an articulate

[42] *Ib.*, xxxiii, 82–90.

language. In all literalness, "the heavens declare the glory of God,"—as a stupendous hieroglyphic. God's universe is his Word translated into images of sense,—frozen theology. So conversely, theology is the master-key to nature; and theological categories are behind the number and ordering of the heavens themselves.

From the unity of God proceeds the Trinity, and from each person thereof proceeds a triad of Intelligences,—the angelic hierarchies; since, as the end of being of these angelic Intelligences is contemplation of God, there must in the divine plenitude be as many degrees and kinds of them as there are logically degrees and kinds of possible contemplation. As God may be contemplated as Father, as Son, as Holy Spirit, so there are three corresponding angelic hierarchies in descending degree. But as each person of the Trinity may also be contemplated either in and for itself alone or in relation to each of the two others, so each of the three hierarchies contains three orders.

Simultaneously created with the nine angelic orders were the nine material heavens. At bottom these are but instruments for transforming the spiritual powers of the angels into physical energies,—just as our bodies effectuate our volitions. The primary effect is the revolution of the heavens both as one whole system and severally. The revolution of the whole system is mechanically involved in that of the outermost material sphere, which is accordingly called the *Primum Mobile*. Being clear of star or planet, it is also called the "crystalline heaven." Each of the eight included spheres has, in addition to the revolution communicated by the *Primum Mobile*, also a lesser and counter revolution of its own. And moreover, each of the seven planets, except the Sun, revolves around a fixed point in its own (already revolving) heaven.

The whole complex of these cyclic and epicyclic movements is the mechanism, the clock-work, we call nature. For Dante, however, the apparent mechanism is throughout really instinct with life and intelligence. The moving power in it and of it all is loving aspiration towards God, its creator. Also, nature is the instrument of divine providence for the salvation of mankind, providing for both his material and spiritual life.[43]

On the model of this cosmos, then accepted scientific fact, Dante shaped the three kingdoms of his mythic other world—paradise, hell, purgatory. Like Plato, he "gives verisimilitude to Myth by making it explain facts, or what he accepts as facts, and bringing it, as far as possible into conformity with the 'modern science' of his day."[44] But Dante's mythic other world, again like Plato's, is intended to have the value of a regulative ideal, not of scientic fact. The distinction is all too commonly blurred—in Dante's case no less than in Plato's.

The fact from which Dante starts is the actual constitution of the heavens according to the Christianized Ptolemaic system. On the model of that he will construct his hell and purgatory, making in their constitutions such amendments of the heavenly scheme as their diverse natures demand. He was profoundly prejudiced in favor of the structural symmetry of things, even asserting it in the face of obvious fact,—as when he makes the Mediterranean extend just ninety degrees, whereas in fact it extends barely forty-two degrees.[45] So he assumes a presumptive symmetry between all three otherworld kingdoms. And thus, although the heavens as correspondent to the angelic orders would naturally be disposed into three groups of three, they are actually otherwise disposed. First there are the seven planetary

[43] Par., viii, 97 ff.
[44] J. A. Stewart: The Myths of Plato, London, 1905, p. 94.
[45] Par., ix, 82–7.

heavens—three of "blame" and four of "honor"—then
the heaven of the fixed stars, then the crystalline heaven,
and finally a wholly disparate heaven, the Empyrean.
In other words, there are seven heavens of one type
succeeded by two somewhat different from the rest and
from each other, and one altogether different. This proportion of 7–2–1 gives Dante a structural formula for
his two other kingdoms. That is, the proportion is kept,
though the units are differently ordered. The terraces of
purgatory proper are seven; below are the two regions
of ante-purgatory; above is the table-land of the earthly
paradise. Again, as the planetary heavens are subdivided
into three of "blame" and four of "honor," so the terraces of purgatory are subdivided into three and four,
in which respectively sins of love disordered in its object or its degree are expiated. Perverted love is expiated
in the three lowest terraces; defective love in the lowest
terrace of the upper four; excessive love in the three
highest terraces.[46] In hell, counting downwards in the
direction of increasing demerit, there is one region outside the gate for the punishment of the morally neuter,—
one just inside the gate for those whose "original sin"
has not been washed away by the water of baptism,—
then four circles for sins of the appetite,—then one for
heretics or those who have rejected Christ,—then three
for wilful sins, this last group being subdivided into one
circle for sins of violence and two for malice, whether
of fraud or treachery.[47] The circles of lower hell are
themselves variously subdivided into "rings" (gironi)
or "ditches" (bolge) for the special sins that make up
the more general classes corresponding to the "circles"
(cerchi). The structure of hell is thus seen to be more
complex than that of either paradise or purgatory, but
close inspection reveals the same proportional formula

[46] Purg., xvii, 112 ff.   [47] Hell, xi

of 7, 2, and 1 as holds for them. The outside region of the neuters is as disparate from the rest of hell as the empyrean is from the other heavens, or the earthly paradise from the rest of the purgatorial mountain. The first and sixth circles really concern theological rather than moral sins, and so group together and apart from the remaining seven assigned to moral sins proper.

To summarize numerically, the formula for paradise, as given by the actual heavens, is (3–4)–2–1; that for purgatory is 2–(3–4)–1; that for hell is 1–1–4–1–3. This analysis may seem tedious, but it is offered as not without value for the understanding of Dante's architectonic methods. For he is far from building on this numerical proportion of the heavens as a bald fact. No facts in nature are for him bald facts; all are significant to such as have eyes to see. He is particularly open-eyed to the symbolic significance of numbers. The symbolism of the *New Life* culminates in the mystic association of Beatrice with the number nine, and there is hint of intention in the curiously symmetrical groupings of the poems themselves.[48] Manifestly intentional repetition of certain numbers in the structure of the *Divine Comedy* has often been noted. Three beasts attack Dante in the dolorous valley; three holy women in heaven intercede for him; three guides lead him from hell to heaven. The verse is *terza rima*, or "rhyme of three." There are three canticles of thirty-three cantos each,—if the first canto of *Hell* may be regarded as introductory to the whole poem. The whole poem thus consists of one hundred cantos, or ten times ten. And, as already said, hell, purgatory, and paradise each has ten divisions. Systematic investigation, from the standpoint of folk-

[48] Originally noted by C. E. Norton. See *The New Life* of Dante (1892), pp. 129–34. His views have been variously combatted and extended.

lore as well as of conscious mysticism, of medieval
number symbolism is still a desideratum. Further information would probably give new and richer significance
to Dante's use of it. Probably, indeed, Aristotle's casual
remark that the Pythagoreans regarded ten as the perfect number was at least in Dante's mind. Again, to a
religious fancy the number three naturally suggests the
Trinity,—as Dante in the New Life declares when by
a virtual pun he explains Beatrice's association with
"nine" as evidence of her divine nature being rooted in
the Trinity.[49] To the religious fancy, also, thirty-three
—the number of cantos in a canticle—might recall the
number of years Christ lived on earth.

Waiving these still largely indeterminate matters,
however, we may return to the more demonstrable and
significant symbolism Dante read out of the actual
Christian-Ptolemaic system of the universe, and so into
his paradise, hell, and purgatory, making these in the
image of that universe—real for him,—as that real universe in its turn was made in the image of the divine
nature.

THE SYMBOLIC STRUCTURE OF PARADISE

As bodies responsive to the nine degrees of angelic
intelligence of God, the heavens would represent a stupendous scala amoris, or ladder of love, raised from
earth to the Empyrean. For intelligence of God, and
love of him, are functions each of the other. We love
in the measure of our knowledge, and we know in the
measure of our knowledge, and we know in the measure of our love. In paradise is the eternal realization
of charity, or love of God, for each according to his
personal merit,—or what is the same, his proved capacity of loving God. The nine heavens then would seem

[49] New Life, xxx.

to offer a kind of thermometer of love. The measure
of love for angels, however, differs from that for men
in so far as human love of God has been developed
and proved in and by the earthly life. Angelic love suf-
fers no change. Human love begins and may end, increases or diminishes, is constant or fickle. Accordingly,
Dante's master, Thomas Aquinas, reduces human love
of God, or charity, to three root degrees,—*incipient, proficient,* and *perfect;* and to three kinds of manifesta-
tion,—of *deed,* of *will,* and of *intellect.*[50] As in the incipient stage of charity there is no appreciable difference of
mode, there result only seven possible separate combina-
tions of mode and degree:—incipient charity; proficient
charity of deed, of will, of intellect; perfect charity of
deed, of will, of intellect. An eighth possible combina-
tion would be collective, or perfection in all three modes
at once. So far the capacity of man as man has been intended. Above such capacity is that of angels, who thus
constitute a ninth degree in the ascending scale of holy
love. And finally, there is the tenth, but really incom-
mensurable, degree of God's own capacity of love.

Patently, in this graded scale of love is reproduced
the exact proportion of the real heavens,—seven relatively similar planetary heavens under two alike in
materiality, though distinct, under one immaterial and
wholly disparate. To "assign," therefore, meritorious
souls to these different heavens, as Dante does, is
merely to indicate the degree and mode of holy love
for which they had proved their capacity on earth. But,
as already said, such assignment is mythic, not scientific. Dante, as with good reason he is careful to say,
does not mean anything like Plato's apparent notion that
souls after death return to their birth-stars.[51] Such a

[50] Cf. G. Busnelli: *Il concetto a l'ordine del "Paradiso" dantesco,* 2 vols., 1911–12.   [51] Par., iv, 28 ff.

doctrine would be flat heresy. He makes, however, symbolic conformity between the spheres and the spiritual merit they severally signify.

Thus over the three lowest heavens reaches in nature the conical shadow of the earth; so likewise over the meritorious spirits assigned to them for Dante's edification there was on earth some shadow of the world and the flesh. In the lowest sphere, the spotted and inconstant Moon, are met as representative of those whose charity in this life had been but inceptive,—nuns recreant under duress, whose secret wills were for God, but their open consent for the world. In Mercury, the humble little planet almost hidden in the greater glory of the Sun,[52] appear with poetic justice those whose charity had been proficient in good works, but whose service towards the glory of God was tinged with the vainglory of worldly ambition. Their spokesman to Dante is Justinian, emperor, codifier of the Roman Law, and restorer by the aid of Belisarius, his captain, of the empire in Italy. In passing, however, it may be said that at this point in his general argument Dante himself needed the dramatic services of Justinian to prove the divine right of the Roman Empire to universal dominion, and so to lead up to the doctrine of the Atonement. There is no evidence presented for holding Justinian particularly worldly in his motives; and it is quite possible that "the Law-Giver's" humble station in heaven is due not so much to Dante's moral judgment as to Dante's literary convenience.

In Venus, highest of the heavens to be touched by the earth's shadow, they appear who had been of great capacity for love, but had taken overmuch as objects of their loving "present things with their false pleasure,"— even as by his own confession had Dante.[53] Venus is

[52] *Ib.*, v. 129.   [53] *Purg.*, xxxi, 34–5.

described in effect as now turning towards, now away from, the Sun.[54] So, it would seem, the ardent spirits met in Venus—Charles Martel, Cunizza of Romano, and the troubadour-bishop Folquet—had greatly loved, but not always God first.

Fittingly, givers of light to men are those who throng the radiant Sun, and of whom the spokesmen are Thomas Aquinas and Bonaventura. Theirs was the intellectual love of God as Truth. Though they had lived without moral flaw—unlike them of the heavens below,— yet in degree their charity had been only proficient, since it was directed not towards God himself but towards his word and Works.[55] The truth they were given to seek and impart was communicable, practicable truth, natural and scriptural revelation mediated for human needs. So by God's will they had been like Martha serviceable, not permitted that "best part" of the contemplative Mary.[56] Their loved object, truth reduced to human comprehensibility, bears the same relation to truth in itself as their sphere, the "sensible Sun," bears to "the Sun of the angels," God in himself.[57] Their merit would be attainment of the "intellectual virtues"— knowledge, wisdom, understanding—by the perfect exercise of human reason; and their merit therefore would be less than that of the spirits of Saturn in degree as knowledge, wisdom, understanding as virtues are inferior to the same as "gifts of the Spirit"; for the virtues derive from man's reason, but the gifts from God's inspiration.[58]

[54] Par., viii, 101–11.   [55] Par., x, 49–51.
[56] Luke, x, 42 (Vulgate).   [57] Par., x, 53–4.
[58] Cf. Aquinas: Summa theol., xlv, 1. "Wisdom posited as a gift of the Holy Spirit differs from wisdom posited as an acquired intellectual virtue; for the latter is acquired by human study, the former is sent down from above." (Cited from W. H. V. Reade: The Moral System of Dante's Inferno, p. 99.)

In the three highest planets are represented manifestations of charity—in deed, will, and intellect—in the perfect degree. Be it repeated that in paradise itself all will evince according to their individual capacities *perfect* charity. The inceptive and proficient grades are but indicative of earthly attainment,—by which attainment, however, rank in heaven is determined. Moreover, as Dante's otherworld is mythic and regulative, not rigidly scientific, his assignments of rank there must be taken as illustrative rather than—even in his own intention— finally judicial. Thus the wisdom of the Sun, as said, is lower in the divine scale than that of Saturn, in so far as the former appertains to the active, the latter to the contemplative, life. The saints and doctors who by Dante are assigned to the Sun must be considered there as preachers of the Word, counsellors of men, even though some named—Hugh of St. Victor, for instance— were actually in life also contemplatives, and so eligible to the higher sphere of Saturn. Also, it is incredible that Dante soberly believed that the heathen Trajan and Ripheus—saved only by a miracle—shall actually stand nearer God than King Solomon or St. Augustine; yet the latter pair appear in the fourth, the former pair in the sixth, heaven.[59] The fact of the matter is that the personages introduced to illustrate logical categories may well be larger than the categories. Indeed, in strict accuracy, every individual blessed spirit, like every angel, loving uniquely, must have its unique place in the heavenly hierarchy. But right understanding of God's plan of reward and punishment is for Dante the thing needful. The human examples he presents to illustrate that plan are no doubt as exact as his judgment and convenience— and perhaps his personal predispositions—allowed; but the really important thing is that they should clearly

[59] Par., xxix, 136–41.

illustrate. In general, they certainly do.

Further to define for Dante the quality of their loves the spirits in Mars, Jupiter, and Saturn show him visible symbols. Arranged constellation-wise as a great white Cross against the red background of the warlike planet Mars, chant God's crusaders, defenders of the Faith against infidel might. Theirs had been perfect charity in deed, as their emblem is remindful of the supreme act of charity, Christ's sacrifice. Against the white and temperate Jupiter flames the ruddy Eagle, emblem of just empire. As Dante had declared in his essay on Monarchy, the business of the divinely ordained emperor is to maintain world-peace, without which mankind cannot attain its end of perfection.[60] Spokesmen in Jupiter are the just rulers of all times. As if to show a true concert of the powers, they speak through the Eagle's beak as one.

Mars and Jupiter represent the perfection of the active life on earth in and for the state. The crystal-clear Saturn, supporting a golden Ladder such as Jacob saw reaching upward illimitably, represents the other and higher perfection of the contemplative life,—that "perfect life and high merit which," as Piccarda says, "emparadises" St. Clare.[61] As they of the three lowest heavens had in life been stained somewhat with the world and the flesh, so by extreme contrast they of Saturn had renounced the world altogether to sink themselves in God. Hermit and monk are their representatives,—Peter Damian and Benedict.

Dante lavishes every device to make this seventh heaven of the contemplatives, perfect in intellectual love, most beautiful. Dante is only voicing the preference, inevitable in Catholic theological consistency, for the contemplative life; but, owing to a prejudice of our

[60] On Monarchy, xi.   [61] Par., iii, 97.

own, we modern readers are likely to misunderstand
him. It is our democratic prejudice that the best is none
too good for anyone, and that all ought to strive for it.
Consequently, the casual reader among us—especially
the non-Catholic reader—may understand Dante to hold
up the contemplative and "religious," the withdrawn,
life as an ideal for all. This is not so. He means that
every man should make his life not the best life,—as
if pigs should try to fly,—but the best life for him. Individual capacity is given. It is for each to make the
best of that gift. So if a man's gift is for the active life,
it would be not meritorious but positively wicked—because insubordinate to God's will—for him to aspire
now and here to the contemplative life, "best" though
that may be in itself.[62] Indeed, as we have seen, behind Dante's own justification for his temporary turning
from Beatrice to the Compassionate Lady was his symbolic identification of the latter with the active life to
which he felt himself called by his gifts as well as perhaps by a special providence.

Above the seven planetary heavens is the starry
heaven. As the first heaven marks the grade of inceptive charity, in which the modes of deed and will and
intellect are not yet to be distinguished, so this eighth—
or highest of the spheres carrying material globes—indi-
cates a charity in which the three modes have reached
the degree of perfection not distributively—as in Mars,
Jupiter, and Saturn—but collectively. A select few of
mankind have realized this superabounding love,—notably Adam, modelled by the divine artist's own hand
and so type of perfect humanity, and also the Apostles,
glorified by personal communion with Christ, the God-
Man.

The collective perfection which these chosen few

[62] Par., viii, 115–48.

among men represent individually, redeemed humanity
in its totality also represents. The stellar heaven therefore exhibits to Dante "the triumph of all the hosts of
Christ,"[63] myriads of lights beneath that central sun.

Fittingly indicative of the grades of human blessedness are the heavens of the planets and stars,—spheres
bearing with them, that is, material bodies. For the
human elect will have bodies hereafter as here, though
then glorified bodies. Angels, on the other hand, are
forever bodiless. So, fittingly again, their triumph is
represented in the ninth heaven, crystalline-clear.

Conceived as above all the material and mobile heavens is the mystic heaven of rest, the Empyrean, sphere
"of pure light intellectual, full of love."[64] As betoken-
ing a creature merit uniquely above that of men or
angels, the Empyrean is by implication represented in
Dante's scale of spiritual values by the Virgin alone
under God.[65] In its eternal actuality, however, the Empyrean is paradise, the one true and real paradise,
one bourne of all the blest. There eternally are they
ranked according to their deserts; and to Dante they
show themselves ordered so upon the petals, tier on
tier, of the symbolic Rose. The Rose itself, capping
the symbols of the Cross, the Eagle, and the Ladder,
expresses the final fruition of holy love in oneness with
God. For the Cross of the Atonement for original sin
signifies initiation into the Christian life; the Eagle of
the supreme civil empire signifies the uplifting and corrective virtues of the active or civil life,—the four cardinal or moral virtues of prudence, justice, fortitude,
and temperance; the Ladder, "scala amoris," signifies
the transcendent and perfecting virtues of the contemplative life,—the three theological or religious virtues of

[63] Par., xxiii, 19–21.   [64] Par., xxx, 39–40.
[65] Ib., xxiii, 136–9.

faith, hope, and charity; the Rose signifies reward of merit so attained, and is the emblem of membership in the Church Triumphant,—even as, in Catholic interpretation, it is the Church who in the *Song of Solomon* cries to the heavenly Bridegroom, "I am the Rose of Sharon."[66]

THE SYMBOLIC STRUCTURE OF HELL

Conformably with his notion of symmetry in nature, Dante's hell in a suggestive way inversely parallels his paradise. Dante is too much of an artist to refine his correspondences too far. But suggestively contraposed to the triune God in his Empyrean, or "fiery heaven," is the three-faced Satan in his prison of ice. In the ninth heaven Dante sees God as a point of intensest brilliancy, centre of nine luminous angelic circles. So Satan, prince of darkness, forms the centre of the nine dark or lurid infernal circles. The symbolic colors of the Trinity as seen by Dante in the mystic triune circle in his final vision,[67] are according to medieval symbolism white, green, and red.[68] White is faith, the light of the Father; green is hope, the ray of the Son; red is love, the splendor of the Holy Spirit.[69] Two of the faces of Satan are also whitish and reddish, but a yellow-white and a muddy red.[70] In him, charity—the desire of good—is all converted to desire of evil. Lost

[66] ii, 1. The ecclesiastical gift of the Golden Rose implies similar reward of merit. In the characteristic symbolic poem of medieval France, The Romance of the Rose, the Rose signifies the object of all desire.

[67] *Par.*, xxxiii, 115–7.

[68] Cf. Busnelli: *Il concetto e l'ordine del "Paradiso" dantesco*, I, 58–9.

[69] For the distinction between "light," "ray," and "splendor," see *Banquet*, III, xiv, 38 ff.

[70] *Hell*, xxxiv, 37–45.

for him is the power which springs from faith; so his sallow face shows his impotence. And in place of green-springing hope, his third face shows the blackness of despair. Once more,—for it would be tedious to dig out too many of these to us merely quaint and ingenious correspondences,—as the faithful disciples are nearest in heaven of men to God, so nearest to Satan in hell is the unfaithful disciple, Judas.[71]

As the heavenly spheres serve Dante as a rising scale of human merit, so the infernal circles are made to correspond likewise to degrees of human demerit. Demerit is due to sins either of inordinate appetite or of perverted will. Victim of his passions, man sinks to the level of the brutes; creature of malice, to that of the fallen angels. Hell, the sphere of punishment, falls accordingly into two grand divisions where are punished respectively sins of incontinence due to infirmity of will and sins of malice due to obliquity of will. Sins of incontinence derive from four root vices,—lust, gluttony, avarice (or the opposite excess, prodigality), and wrath. Sins of malice involve injury as their end. There may be injury by force or by fraud. There may be fraud without breach of trust, or with it.

Counting sins of malice as thus threefold, we reach seven classes of sin altogether. Besides these seven sins personal to the sinner, however, there is also according to Christian belief another sin common to mankind. This is "original sin,"—the sin of Adam visited upon all from generation to generation. This original sin can be expiated in but one way,—participation in the Atonement through baptism. Non-participation must be due either to inability or to perversity.

When Dante makes the virtuous Virgil—naturally unable to believe in the Christ he could not know—affirm

[71] Ib., xxxiv, 61–3.

that he and those like him "sinned not," Dante does not mean that they were without sin.[72] On the contrary, as Virgil himself elsewhere declares, he was to be forever punished in Limbo for "original sin:"

> There I abide with little innocents
> Who have been bitten by the teeth of Death
> Before they were exempt from human sin.[73]

Punishment for such "invincible ignorance" is contrary to justice as human reason sees it, but is a necessary article of Catholic faith.[74] To fit the negative guilt, however, punishment for invincible ignorance must be merely privative. The individual heathen as a man may be quite humanly perfect, his appetite and will wholly governed by reason. What his will lacks to move it to God is not reason but revelation. Thus Limbo, his place of punishment, is collocated with the circles of sins of incontinence—in which the will of the sinner lacked control of reason,—yet somewhat apart from and above them. The torment of its denizens is the consciousness of the might-have-been.

Within Limbo itself there are two regions, one dark, the other relatively bright. Both belong to the invincibly ignorant; but only the bright region with its noble castle is of the truly wise and virtuous of old, who before the saving light of Christ lived as best they could by the pale light of unaided reason. To such as they, Dante also declares, the divine mercy has indeed from time to time been miraculously extended. Christ himself rescued, when he descended into hell, the virtuous of Israel who were taught by their prophets to believe in the Messiah to come. The Emperor Trajan, agrees Dante, was miraculously restored to life long enough to

[72] *Hell*, iv, 34. [73] *Purg.*, vii, 31–3.
[74] *Par.*, xix, 70 ff.

receive the sacrament; the Trojan Ripheus, as told in the *Aeneid*, led a life so just, so imbued with the very spirit of Christ, that he may be said to have had an instinct of Christ to come, an implicit faith.[75] Cato also, if we may judge by his stern contrasting of his own position with that of his wife Marcia "beyond the evil stream" of Acheron, is to be saved. And Virgil is at least promised Beatrice's intercession in heaven.[76] In so leaning to hopefulness for divine mercy towards virtuous ancients, Dante expresses not only his own predisposition in their favor, but also the doctrine of St. Thomas.[77]

The second obstacle to saving acceptance of the faith, wilful ignorance of God, is a sin against the light. The heretic who refuses the saving truth is indeed morally stiffnecked, though in all other respects he may be virtuous, and for obliquity of will is punished in the lower hell, within the city of Dis; yet since he may be without violence or fraud, his circle is on a plane above the nether abyss. As associated with pride, on the other hand, the circle of the heresiarchs is fitly next below that of wrath, for pride follows wrath in Dante's ordering of the capital vices.

Thus hell has an upper abyss of five circles, a nether and double abyss of four. The uppermost circle of each group is distinct from the rest of the group, and the two are structurally analogous to each other.

Of the seven circles of moral sins proper, only four strictly correspond to the so-called capital vices. In fact, as he explains in the eleventh canto, Dante classifies moral sins upon a twofold basis roughly after Aristotle.[78]

[75] *Par.*, xx.   [76] *Hell*, ii, 73–4.
[77] Cf. Aquinas: *Summa theol.*, I-II, lxxvi, 2.
[78] Aristotle has a third category,—sins of bestiality. These, however, Dante apparently merges with sins of injury by violence in the seventh circle. Cf. W. H. V. Reade: *The Moral System of Dante's Inferno*, chap. xxiv.

As said above, there are sins of uncontrolled appetite, or incontinence, and sins of perverted will, or malice. In the former there is defect of reason; in the latter obliquity of reason.

These seven circles, themselves subdivided into "rings" and "ditches" for the several species of the major sins, are supplemented by two more circles for the theological sins of defect of faith and rejection of faith of the unbaptized and heretics respectively.

To these nine internal regions of hell Dante adds a tenth and external region, so completing the structural analogy with the nine graded material heavens capped by the disparate tenth heaven, or Empyrean.

This tenth infernal region, as a place of eternal punishment yet outside hell, corresponds to a moral category apparently of Dante's own invention, though perhaps suggested by the vice of pusillanimity in Aristotle's scheme.[79] Obviously there must also have been in Dante's mind the condemnation of the Laodiceans,— "Because thou art lukewarm, and neither hot nor cold, I will spue thee out of my mouth,"[80] as well as the warning of Christ that "He that is not with me is against me."[81]

The "caitiff choir" assigned to this purlieu of hell is damned not for demerit, whether of original or of personal sin, but for defect of merit, for failure to contribute their necessary share towards their own redemption. God helps those—and only those—who help themselves. If heaven excludes them for lack of merit, hell excludes them for lack of demerit. Will-less either for good or for evil, they may in a purely negative sense be called innocent, without sin; but they are also

---

[79] Cf. Reade, op. cit., pp. 395 et seq. Connection with the medieval vice of accidia, or moral inertia, is also arguable.

[80] Rev., iii, 16.   [81] Matt., xii, 30.

without virtue. As even negatively speaking innocent, however, their state has in so far a certain analogy to that of the blessed in the Empyrean and of the purified in Eden. So they occupy a region outside and above their kingdom of hell, as the Empyrean transcends the material universe and Eden tops the mount of purgatory. But the innocence of the earthly paradise and heavenly paradise is vital; the innocence of the caitiffs is lethal. They were never truly alive;[82] for to live is to will,—which they could not. As if in grim parody of the joyous circling of the angels around the throne of God, the caitiffs in their faint light and confused hubbub go round and round in a circle aimlessly forever.[83]

The Symbolic Structure of Purgatory

In that it involves a turning away from imperishable to perishable good, every sin has in it two elements. Aquinas calls these two elements "aversion" and "conversion."[84] Aversion from imperishable good or God is the formal element of all sin, and the essential disposition of the damned in hell. To escape damnation every sinner must therefore first of all overcome that "aversion,"—or in other words, repent. Repentance at once reunites the will to God as the true end of desire, but does not wholly remove the material element of the sin, namely, "inordinate conversion to perishable good." In spite of the good intention of the sinner, his passions may—so long as he remains in the flesh—still be inordinately moved by "perishable good," his reason err as to secondary ends.

[82] Cf. Hell, iii, 64.

[83] Ib., iii, 52–7. Cf. Par., xxviii, 25 ff.

[84] ". . . in peccato autem duo sunt, quorum unum est aversio ab incommutabili bono . . . aliud quod est in peccato est inordinata conversio ad commutabile bonum." Summa theol., I-II, lxxxvii, 4.

Dante's desire, for instance, though his ultimate intention was always towards Beatrice, was temporarily drawn aside by "present things with their false pleasure."[85] Such lapses may be atoned for by penance. But death may—virtually always does—prevent complete penance. "Relics of sin" (reliquiae peccati) are then left in the soul, which must be washed away in purgatory. In the soul that is admitted into purgatory there is indeed no active virus of sin left, no "malice"; that soul can no longer lapse through any temptation;[86] its sin has become external to it, leaving only such a mark as the crusted skin left by a fever. Purgatory then is a place of the spirit's convalescence, a place— if the term may be allowed—of moral "peeling." The penitent is made presentable for the society of the blest. Purgatorial penance is neither merely a vindictive exaction by a jealous God, nor yet a further testing and proving of the soul. The opportunity of complete atonement offered by purgatory is both an imposition of divine justice and a signal act of divine mercy. It is how divine mercy permits divine justice to be satisfied. Purgatory is in fact a corollary of Christ's Atonement, before which, according to Dante, penitent souls had to await in Limbo the Saviour's coming.

Since purgatory thus exists only by the grace of God through Christ, it is open only to such as have received grace. Of his own volition man may repent of sin, but only by divine aid is his repentance made efficacious for purification from sin. And divine aid is given to the Christian in the sacrament of the Church, God's vicar.

[85] Purg., xxxi, 34–5.

[86] On the first cornice above the entrance-gate of purgatory, the shades of the proud say the Lord's Prayer, excluding—as irrelevant to themselves—the petition, "Lead us not into temptation." Purg., xi, 19–24.

Now if a sinner repent, he is saved from hell. Yet without divine aid he cannot enter purgatory, the obligatory gateway to paradise. Suppose the Church for reason withhold the necessary sacrament? Suppose the sinner put off repentance to his latest breath?

Answering these two hypothetical questions, Dante is brought to recognize two special classes of penitents, who are, so to speak, provisionally redeemable. Their repentance, while it saves them from hell, is incompetent to pass them after death along with the normally absolved others at once into purgatory. In being presently ineligible for either hell or heaven they are like the "caitiffs"; only, whereas the "caitiffs" remain eternally ineligible, these are but temporarily so.

In the person of Manfred Dante presents the extreme case of present ineligibility for purgatory. Manfred has been guilty of mortal sin, has been excommunicated and never absolved, and yet with his last breath repents.[87] Without hesitation Dante promises ultimate redemption to such a man. For had the Church known in time of the man's repentance, her ban must by sacred right have been lifted, and the sacrament given. Such is God's declared and merciful will. So, as it is inconceivable that God's will should be thwarted by a dying penitent's physical disability to reach the Church, the sacrament may be regarded as implicitly given.[88]

But from such a penitent manifestly excess penance is due. Before opportunity is given to purge the relics of other sins, satisfaction must be rendered both for the contumacy of rejecting the grace of God through his Church and the negligence of repentance postponed. Dante rules that this penitent must wait outside purgatory-gate thirty times the duration of his obduracy.

Where, on the other hand, there is remissness in late

[87] Purg., iii. [88] Ib., iii, 124–9.

repentance without contumacy,—mere dilatoriness, in other words,—the penalty of delay is but thrice the duration of remissness, and also upon the slope of the mount, instead of at its very base.

Thus are constituted by logical necessity two regions purgatorial in character, and yet below the gate of purgatory proper. In this ante-purgatory temptation to evil still assails the yet imperfectly eligible penitent. The peril is met, however, by the penitent's instant appeal for divine aid, which is as quickly granted.

This interregnal state between the spiritual precariousness of earthly life and the assured confidence of purgatory itself is symbolized by the invasion at nightfall of Eve's tempter, the Serpent, the appeal of the affrighted shades in the psalm *Te lucis ante*, and the coming of the guardian angels.[89] Dante's own admission into purgatory, as effected by grace given and accepted, is doubly symbolized. He sleeps, and dreams of being carried by an eagle into a sphere of fire. On awakening, he learns from Virgil that he has actually been transported by St. Lucy to the gate of purgatory. As several times in the *Divine Comedy*, the dream is a presage of immediately consequent happenings. Lucy, whose name from *lux* implies "light," and for whom in effect the shades in their psalm *Te lucis ante* had prayed, signifies the "illuminating grace" which alone makes repentance efficacious. The "eagle" may perhaps stand for that "spark" (*scintilla*) of the divine in the human soul which kindles the fires of charity, and which Aquinas calls *synderesis*, and likens for its aspiring and uplifting power to an eagle.[90] Certainly, Dante

[89] *Purg.*, viii.

[90] *Sent.*, II, xxiv, 3. On *synderesis* as *scintilla*, see *Ib.*, II, xxxix, 3. In the present connection Dante introduces the figure of a lantern. *Purg.*, viii, 112.

hints strongly at the allegorical importance of this particular bit of action:

> Here, reader, sharpen well thine eyes for truth;
> Surely the veil is now so thin indeed
> That it is easy to pass through within.[91]

As purgatory is, as said, an uniquely Christian place of expiation, the order of sins in it is naturally according to Christian philosophy. There are then seven regions corresponding to the seven capital vices, from which as from roots, all vices grow,—namely, in ascending order from purgatory-gate, rounds (*gironi*) or terraces for the purgation of pride, envy, anger, sloth, avarice (or prodigality), gluttony, lust. Properly speaking, however, it is not these vices themselves that the souls in purgatory are purging, but only "relics" or scars of them. A residuum of actual vice in the soul must involve temptation and possible lapse, and, as already said, to neither of these is the soul once within the gate of purgatory subject.

When with the aid of God the penitent soul has rid itself of its scars,—when the angel has erased the last "P" (for *peccatum*) from Dante's brow,—each again becomes what man was fresh from his Maker's hands—type and perfection of human kind. Eden is regained.

So the tenth region of Dante's purgatory is in fact the Garden of Eden, earthly counterpart of the tenth heaven, or true paradise. So is the lost Eden regained by every Christian saved, who on the way of becoming as the angels who fell not passes through the condition of Adam before his fall. Thus in effect mankind actually rises to its heavenly home from Eden, as God in the beginning willed.

At the base of the mount before the dawn of his first

[91] Purg., viii, 19–21.

day in purgatory Dante saw four stars; just below purgatory-gate after dusk of that day he saw three more.[92]
In Eden these seven stars take on human form as
handmaids of Beatrice, aids to blessedness, the seven
virtues, moral and theological.[93] Ministered unto by all
seven and formally shriven of all relics of sin, Dante
lacks no means of attainment of the heavenly Beatrice
save passage through the portal of death. Naturally, the
pilgrim of the Divine Comedy does not actually pass
this portal, but is, as we have seen, temporarily and
miraculously transfigured (trasumanato) in the false
death of the mystic's ecstasy.

SECONDARY SYMBOLISM OF THE THREE KINGDOMS

Dante thus constructed his mythic three kingdoms on
the architectural model of the ten heavens of accepted
medieval astronomy, modified to conform symbolically
to the categorical divisions of orthodox theology and
ethics. For his symbolic paradise indeed, he simply took
over the actual heavens; but hell and purgatory he had
for himself to shape and localize. And here again not
pure fantasy seeking the dramatic and picturesque, but
strict symbolic logic was his organon.

God for Dante is transcendent, outside his universe,
and no "spirit interfused"—except through angelic inter-
mediaries. If we imaginatively conceive God's heaven
as tangential at every point to the material outer globe
of the universe, the farthest point in every direction
from God is the centre of the earth. Here therefore
should be the seat of Satan, spiritual opposite of God.
Since Satan is unique in his evil, no one else can be on
just his plane of punishment; therefore hell must ter-
minate in him as in a point. To have reached the cen-

[92] Purg., i, 22–7; viii, 85–93.   [93] Ib., xxxi, 106–8.

tre of the earth, Satan must have crashed through the earth-crust in his fall from heaven; and, considered as a projectile, must have ploughed through, heaving up the crust behind him. This heaved-up crust forms the island of purgatory, midmost point of the hemisphere of water and directly antipodal to Jerusalem. Thus the myth of Satan's literal fall, so extended, would make him dig his own everlasting grave, and also in the same act raise the mount by which men may escape from him back to heaven. So Satan willy-nilly has fulfilled God's purposes and defeated his own. Incidentally, that Dante desires this explanation of the site of hell to be taken as symbolic myth and not literal fact,—however much he may plausibly conform myth to fact,—is indicated by the word "perhaps" in his account of it.[94]

Symbolic fitness in hell as a prison-hole and purgatory a sky-scaling peak further justifies this mythical genesis. No better instance is there of that happy union of realism and symbolism which constitutes Dante's art than this creation and segregation of hell and purgatory by one mythic act. Previously, localization of both other world kingdoms was vague enough. Purgatory seems generally to have been supposed "a sort of cavern in the bowels of the earth, in the purlieus of hell."[95] Symbolically regarded, such a view would be flagrantly inadequate. It would bind purgatory with hell instead of heaven, and suggest the perfecting penance to be merely punitive. Association of purgatory with divine mercy and grace would be lost, and visualization of it as the climb to last perfection; whereas from the moment the pilgrims in the Divine Comedy emerge from the murky subterranean depths of hell, all physical nature con-

[94] Hell, xxxiv, 121–6.
[95] Cf. P. H. Wicksteed; Dante and Aquinas, London, 1913, p. 213.

spires to comfort and encourage. In the still dawn-dusk of Easter Sunday, at the foot of the mount they see again the stars of hope. The mountain climbed, they stand on its sun-lit, bower-like top—

Pure and disposed to leap unto the stars.[96]

No less exquisitely appropriate again is the setting of the lost Eden upon the top of the island mount. For its sin, mankind lost Eden. Its sin atoned for, mankind regains Eden. God's first will and man's final good are reasserted against the machinations of the fiend.

The physical background of hell, purgatory, and paradise everywhere nicely reflects the spiritual drama. Incident and action of the drama itself are also richly and subtly meaningful. In describing hell and heaven, Dante has not, like so many medieval preachers and poets, merely piled horror upon horror indiscriminate, or hyperbolic bliss on bliss. Each "punishment fits the crime"; each reward the merit. Indeed, we may go further. Each punishment and reward is—at least in suggestion—not something foreign to the spiritual state involved, but that spiritual state itself in symbolic terms. Thus the flaming of the Empyrean, or "heaven of fire," is the vital fire of love; the ice-rack of Satan is his frozenness of heart. The murky blast on which are whirled Francesca da Rimini and her lover is the blind gust of passion on which they were swept into sin. The "noble castle" of the wise and virtuous pagans in Limbo, with its "open, luminous and lofty" garden, yet on all sides hemmed in by the murk of hell, is very type of the well-meaning human mind without grace. So in purgatory the penitents bend low under the pride they had thought to exalt them, or grope about in the

[96] *Purg.*, xxxiii, 145.

gross and bitter fog of wrath that had in life choked and blinded them, or thirst and burn in the fire of lust that had once inflamed their hearts. Since the bliss of love responsive is the one reward of heaven, difference there can exist only in degree. As Dante rises from sphere to sphere, he sees first against the pallid Moon spirits faintly luminous—like a pearl against a woman's white forehead; then in Mercury he sees a spirit so glow with love that the light of its countenance wraps and hides it like a fiery garment. In the higher spheres this self-concealing glory is always over the spirits. Yet more luminous with joy, they appear to Dante only as flaming "gems," "torches," "suns,"—even as the source of their radiancy, God, is seen at last as a focus of light inexpressibly intense.

Like a cameo-worker, Dante overlays symbol on symbol in his pattern. The *Purgatory* is especially so richly stratified in meaning. At bottom is the general topographical symbolism of the Christian moral life, as explained by Dante himself in the seventeenth canto. Superimposed on this development are the three allegorical dreams experienced by him on his three nights on the mount. These allegories express in order the fundamental conflict and the twofold triumph of the Christian moral life. They are the dream below purgatory gate of the Eagle,[97] that on the fourth terrace of the Siren,[98] and that just below the earthly paradise of the sisters Leah and Rachel.[99] In position as well as in significance they thus mark the three crises of the action. In the "Eagle" is symbolized the upward-striving impulse of conscience, the moral instinct—*synderesis* in scholastic terminology—which, aided by illuminating grace, represented by St. Lucy, is able at last to see

[97] *Purg.*, ix.   [98] *Ib.*, xix.
[99] *Ib.*, xxvii, 94 ff.

through the painted siren of vice, so seeming fair, so really foul. So the first two dreams show the casting off of the siren, and the Christian's victory. In the third dream the reward of the victor is indicated by the appearance to him of the two sisters, one typifying perfection in the active life, the other typifying perfection in the contemplative life. Thus these three visions correspond in principle to the four signs in the heavens,—the Eagle, the Cross, the Ladder, the Rose. For these are also signs set before men to guide them in the struggle towards redemption. The Eagle, which in the dream on purgatory mount had stood for private conscience, now also, identified with the Roman Eagle, stands for the right public conscience or civil governance of mankind by the Holy Roman Empire; and the Cross points to the Holy Roman Church as the spiritual guide of men. Also, the Cross and the Ladder together imply the true way of life by sacrifice and aspiration, while the Rose expresses the beauty and fragrance of the life immortal.

Again, overlaid upon the plan of the seven terraces of the seven deadly vices is the symbolism of the seven beatitudes sung by angel guardians, and pointing to virtues corrective of the seven vices. And still further— as if to make assurance of his lesson trebly sure— Dante adds examples from ancient history and scripture of each vice and contrary virtue in the "speech visible" of the *intaglios* of the terrace of pride, in the "speech invisible" of the voices of the terrace of envy, in the dreams of the terrace of wrath, in the exclamations of the penitent chorus on the terraces of sloth and of lust, and of a single penitent on the terrace of avarice, in the mysterious voices from the two trees of the terrace of gluttony.

LITURGICAL SYMBOLISM IN THE DIVINE COMEDY

Liturgical references and allusions are obvious enough in many places of the *Divine Comedy*, especially in the *Purgatory*. Dante climbs the lower slopes of the mountain all of Easter-day. The spirits in this antepurgatory are still—constructively at least—in the sphere of trial and possible failure. They are still of the Church Militant, crying out for mercy, for aid against Satan the old adversary. Dante hears them reciting the regular office of the Church for sext,[100] for vespers,[101] for compline.[102] Once admitted by the angel, however, the penitent soul is safe. No power of evil can reach it now. It has only to cleanse itself of the grime of past sin before entering into the presence of God, and enjoying that intimacy of communion with God which is its reward. Yet the immediate goal of the pilgrim spirit is the earthly paradise. By a beautiful fiction—which for him is in principle truth—Dante so justifies the original design of God temporarily thwarted by the disobedience of man in his unchastened freedom. The elect of the sons of Adam return to the pristine estate of the first father, thence to be recruited into the ranks left empty by the rebel angels. To Adam in Eden God revealed himself visibly. So to Dante in the earthly paradise God reveals himself in Beatrice. But as the earthly paradise symbolizes the perfect life on earth, so Dante's vicarious knowledge of God through Beatrice corresponds with the Christian's vicarious knowledge of God through Christ. And this Christian knowledge of God is on earth mystically fulfilled in the sacrament of the eucharist, by which the communicant is made one in flesh and blood with

[100] *Purg.*, v, 24.   [101] *Ib.*, vii, 82.
[102] *Ib.*, viii, 13.

Christ. There is evident invitation, therefore, to associate symbolically the function of Beatrice in the earthly paradise with the function of the eucharist in the Christian life; and to the limits of congruity Dante accepted the invitation.[103] Suggestive of the veiled monstrance of the Host borne in *Corpus Christi* processions is the veiled maiden borne upon the chariot of the Church, drawn by the two-natured Griffin symbolizing Christ, attended by angels and the Seven Virtues in the guise of dancing maidens, convoyed by the Beasts of the Apocalypse and by the four and twenty paired elders symbolizing the books of the Old and New Testaments, and bearing the holy candelabrum and banners. It is Christ's army in action; and for Dante and his contemporaries there can be no doubt of the sacrament of the eucharist standing as the very palladium—or to use the analogy not unlikely to be in Dante's own mind, the Florentine *carroccio*, or warchariot, the rallying centre of that army. It is noteworthy also that just before the appearance of Beatrice, angels sing *Benedictus qui venis*, manifest adaptation of the *Benedictus qui venit in nomine Domini* chanted in Dante's day, as ever since, in the ordinary of the Mass just before the elevation of the Host.

Dante's sojourn in the earthly paradise covers the forenoon of his fourth day on the island of purgatory. On the second day he had heard the spirits recite the *Te Deum* at matins, and the *Agnus Dei* at vespers,— the former in rejoicing for their escape from hell, the latter in contrition for their past sins. On the third

[103] For this important suggestion I am indebted to Miss Lizette A. Fisher of Columbia University. Her book, *The Vision of God in Grail Legend and Divine Comedy* is, I trust, presently forthcoming. I have followed out the communicated idea in my own way here, and cannot hold her responsible for the arguments advanced.

day the appropriate divine offices are recited at nearly
all the canonical hours.[104] The texts chanted have moreover a progressive significance corresponding to the purgatorial action—from the contrite *Adhaesit pavimento
anima mea* of early morning to the triumphant *Venite,
benedicti Patris mei* of eventide, when from the fire
Dante emerges purged clean. The service of the Mass
is likewise purificatory. It is also notable that the
greater number of the texts chosen by Dante form part
still of the ordinary of the Mass.[105] And again in the
phrases of the "ordinary" "*panem coelestem accipiam*"
and "*calicem salutaris accipiam*" there is striking cor-
respondence with Dante's constant use of the terms
"bread of angels" and "*salute*" (salvation) for the
spiritual pabulum and redemption of the Christian.
Salute—in both senses of the Italian word, the original
"salutation" and the final "salvation"—was, as we have
seen, the gift of Beatrice in the *New Life* as well as
in the *Divine Comedy*; and the "bread of angels,"
which is wisdom, accounts for the title of the *Banquet*,
and is more than once alluded to in the *Divine Comedy*.[106] Both ideas occur together in connection with his
culminating experience in the earthly paradise, where—

> . . . full of awe and happiness, my soul
> Was tasting of the food, which of itself
> Quenching the thirst, arouses thirst anew.[107]

And when Virgil vanishes, just after the appearance of
Beatrice, Dante speaks of him as one

[104] Prime—*Purg.*, xix, 73; terce—xx, 136; sext—xxiii, 11; nones
—xxv, 121; vespers—xxvii, 58.

[105] *Agnus Dei* (*Purg.*, xvi, 19); *Gloria in excelsis Deo* (xx,
136); *Labia mea* (xxiii, 11); *Benedictus qui venis* [for *venit*] (xxx,
19); *Asperges me* (xxxi, 98); also Beatrice's echo of the words of
Christ—*Modicum, et non videbitis me*, &c (xxxiii, 10–12).

[106] *E. g., Purg.*, xxxi, 128–9; *Par.*, ii, 11, xxiv, 1–6.

[107] *Purg.*, xxxi, 128–9.

> . . . to whom for my salvation [*salute*], I
> Had given myself.[108]

Virgil was only Beatrice's agent. It was she, as he again testifies in his final prayer to her, who truly had condescended to bring him salvation:

> O Lady, thou in whom my hope is strong,
> And who for my salvation [*salute*] didst endure
> To leave in hell the footsteps of thy feet. . .[109]

If it be true that Dante by secondary symbolization identified his communion with Beatrice in the earthly paradise with the sacrament of the eucharist, the culminating experience of the *Purgatory* exactly presages that of the *Paradise*. In the *Paradise* Dante attains momentarily the fruition of Christian desire, the "vision of God" or direct intellectual possession of the divine essence. At the close of the *Purgatory* he had received symbolically in the descent to him of Beatrice that which of God's essence the communicant receives in the bread and wine,—mystic possession of Christ through faith. The two implied degrees of reward are those of St. Paul's words: "For now we see through a glass darkly; but then face to face: now I know in part; but then shall I know even as also I am known."[110]

APOCALYPTIC SYMBOLISM IN THE DIVINE COMEDY

> Ye have the Old and the New Testament,
> And of the Church the Shepherd is your guide;
> For your salvation deem ye this enough.[111]

In these words Beatrice epitomizes the faith of the thirteenth century. By Christ's Atonement mankind had

---

108 *Ib.*, xxx, 51–2.   109 *Par.*, xxxi, 79–81.
110 I Cor., xiii, 12.   111 *Par.*, v, 76–8.

been made reëligible for heaven, but was still too en-
ervated by original sin to rise thither unaided. For aid
and comfort God had accordingly given strengthening
truth and wisdom in the Bible, and had inspired his
appointed vicar, the Pope, to interpret the Bible to
blinder men. Moreover, that mankind might pursue its
high aim effectively, God had also set over it another
chosen man, the Emperor, to keep the peace among
the nations of men and to direct earthly activities. Pope
and Emperor, Church and State, were in God's intention to supplement each the other's service for good, as
Mary and Martha together waited upon the Lord, or
as perfection in the active life and in the contemplative
life together sum Christian perfection.

Unhappily, even as Adam in his free will seemed
to thwart God's original beneficent plan, so Pope and
Emperor in their human privilege to err seemed again
to thwart Christ's plan of redemption. The weapons
given them as allies against Satan, they had turned
against each other in mutual jealousy and greed. And
Dante saw in his own time the apparently resulting ca-
tastrophe of the majestic Empire impotently prostrate
and of Holy Church self-profaned and self-defeated in
her own unholy triumph. Against her the three "blasts
from Suabia"—the Hohenstaufen Emperors—had spent
their fury in vain; but

> Say henceforth that the Church of Rome confounds
> Two powers in herself, and in the mire
> Fallen, defiles her burden and herself.[112]

For Dante the original curse of the Church lay in the
"fatal gift" of Constantine,—temporal possessions that
raised in her the thirst of worldly power.[113] *Corruptio
optimi pessima*. Worshippers of the Beast, the she-wolf

[112] *Purg.*, xvi, 127–9.   [113] *Hell*, xix, 115–7.

of cupidity,[114] the two dominant Popes of Dante's time—
Boniface VIII and Clement V—served not Christ but
Anti-Christ. Heaven itself reddens with anger at thought
of them; and St. Peter declares that in the sight of God
his seat on earth is vacant.[115] Gentle Beatrice by her last
words to her lover consigns them to hell.[116]

As St. Peter angrily declares, a pope like each of
these is a "usurper," who

> Has of my cemetery made a sewer
> > Of blood and filth, with which he, the perverse,
> > Who fell from here on high, down there is pleased.[117]

[114] There are five references to "cupidity" [*cupidigia*] in the
Divine Comedy—*Hell*, xii, 49; *Purg.*, vi, 104; *Par.*, v, 79; xxvii,
121; xxx, 139; and these passages seem to have a progressive correlation. In *Hell*, xii, 49–51, Virgil briefly denounces "cupidity"
as the great spur to human wickedness and folly. In *Purg.*, vi,
103–5 Sordello ascribes to the "cupidity" of the Emperors Ru-
dolph and Albert their laying waste of the garden of the Empire.
In *Par.*, v, 79–8, Beatrice makes "cupidity" the primary cause of
disobedience to Holy Church, and so of the thwarting of God's
plan of redemption. Yet it is not strange, as later (*Par.*, xxvii,
121–48) she bitterly declares, that ordinary men should succumb
to a vice before which Pope and Emperor alike have abdicated.
And her indignant last words are to consign to hell Pope Clement
V for having in his "cupidity" betrayed Henry of Luxembourg,
the one recent emperor who had manfully tried to fulfil his responsibility under God (*Par.*, xxx, 133–48). Indeed, in this passage we are shown Henry, as representative of rightful and right
governance, warring against "cupidity." So in his intention at
least, he is one with the "Hound" of *Hell*, i, 101. And whoever
after him shall yet come to hunt the "she-wolf" back to hell more
fortunately, must like Henry know her by the name of "cupidity."

Identification of the symbolic "she-wolf" with the vice of
"cupidity" does not at all necessarily imply that Dante was in any
peculiar sense prone to that vice. As the above cited passages
show, "cupidity" was regarded by Dante as the worst stumbling-
block in the path of the Christian pilgrim of every degree.
Whether or not the "Dante" of the *Divine Comedy* exactly reflects the real Dante or not, the latter would hardly exempt himself from the universal peril of perils.

[115] *Par.*, xxvii, 19–27.   [116] *Ib.*, xxx, 145–8.
[117] *Ib.*, xxvii, 25–7.

Such a pope is representative on earth not of God, but of the Beast of the Apocalypse, and "deceiveth them that dwell on the earth by the means of those miracles which he had power to do in the sight of the beast."[118] And as, according to St. John, that Beast is to be known by a mystic number, which is "of a man," and is "Six hundred threescore and six," so in the same apocalyptic manner Beatrice prophesies another number—"A five hundred, ten and five"—to be that also "of a man" who shall be sent by God to

> slay with her who has usurped
> The giant who is sharer in her sin.[119]

Thus in each of Dante's two apocalyptic prophecies a Beast evilly dominating the world is to be slain and sent down to the hell it serves and deserves. Virgil's prophecy, expressive of the merely human insight he typifies, is vague and nearly indefinite,—a hound born "between Feltro and Feltro" shall harry the she-wolf of cupidity.[120] Beatrice with her insight of Christian revelation, echoes and applies the more (seemingly) precise though presently enigmatic announcements of the Evangelist.

From the context of Beatrice's words, it is plain that the bestial harlot, the Scarlet Woman of the Apocalypse, here identified with the Beast—for such symbolic fusions are in Dante's manner—is the corrupted papacy, and the Giant her paramour, is the anti-imperialist power of France. Naturally, then, the Hound and the "Five Hundred, Ten and Five" would be a Holy Roman Emperor. Since the Pope has turned his God-given power against God, God will turn the coördinate

[118] *Rev.*, xiii, 14.   [119] *Purg.*, xxxiii, 44-5.
[120] *Hell*, i, 94 ff. Dante himself recalls the prophecy in *Purg.*, xx, 10-5.

power of the Emperor against the Pope—or rather
Anti-Pope. So Dante, faithful son of the Church though
he proclaims himself, justifies in so far Ghibellinism.
Unquestionably, he had hoped to find in the Emperor
Henry VII the God-sent "leader"—the DVX, or DXV
("five hundred, ten, and five") transposed; and in reward for Henry's perseverance unto death in his sacred
mission he assigns to the hero one of the few remaining
vacant thrones of the Rose.[121] For Henry's success, as it
proved, the time was unripe;[122] and possibly, Virgil's
obscure hint that the deliverer shall be born "between
Feltro and Feltro[123] may mean that Dante had trans-
ferred his hope to his patron, the young Can Grande
della Scala, chief representative of the Imperialist power
in Italy.

It seems hardly likely, however, that Dante enter-
tained serious hope of any lasting reign of peace on
earth. He declares this world to be in "its last age."[124]
He found the celestial thrones almost all filled. Indeed,
he may even have estimated the remaining years of
mortal existence as just five hundred from the year
1300. Cunizza declares that of her companion in the
heaven of Venus, Folco of Marseilles,

> Great fame was left behind, and ere it die
> This hundredth year shall come a fifth time yet.[125]

According to Adam's statements to Dante,[126] Christ was
born in the year 5200 of the world; the year 1300 would
therefore be the year 6500 of the world; and five hundred years more would make an even seven thousand.
In the medieval symbolism of numbers, seven—union
of the triad and quadrate, or the fourfold principle of

[121] *Par.*, xxx, 130–8.   [122] *Ib.*, xxx, 138.
[123] *Hell*, i, 105.   [124] *Banquet*, II, xv, 115–8.
[125] *Par.*, ix, 39–40.   [126] *Ib.*, xxvi, 118–23.

the elements in conjunction with the threefold principle of the Trinity—is sometimes made to represent nature. In view of this fact and of Dante's boldly schematic simplifications of chronology and geography generally, I venture to infer that he actually counted the sum of the years of the world as just seven thousand. Certainly, a generation which found no incongruity in the precise prophetic chronology of a Joachim of the Flower would not balk at such grandiose reckonings. In any case, the positiveness of Dante's conviction that the world was hurrying to its degenerate end explains much of his pessimism concerning the affairs of life in his day and to come, and his bitterness towards so many of his fellowmen. It need not be, as is sometimes intimated, that he had merely a personal grievance against some of them, but that they were for the most part a lost remnant, fated to be damned, and therefore on theological principles deserving of damnation. Their fate is by God's will; and to willing and loving concurrence with God's will the whole teaching of the *Divine Comedy* converges. Rigorously speaking, therefore, Dante's cold vindictiveness towards Filippo Argenti is prompted by Christian charity, the identification of his own will with God's. Virgil not only commends his scorn—

> Disdainful soul,
> Blessed is she who bore thee in her bosom!—

but promises the satisfaction of Dante's quite proper desire to see the wretch still further tormented. The promise realized, Dante devoutly praises and thanks God.[127] Even more repugnant to modern sensibilities is Dante's tearing out the hair of Bocca degli Abbati, locked helplessly neck-deep in the ice, for refusing to

[127] *Hell*, viii, 31–63.

tell his name.[128] Yet Virgil, who but a little before had been prompt enough to rebuke his charge for mere vulgar curiosity in pausing to listen to the bickerings of the accurst shades, has no word of reproof for this inhumanity. That which God has condemned man has no right to condone. Possibly, in these two particular instances, Dante may have tended to identify God's will with his own rather than his own will with God's,—for he seems to have had grounds of personal animosity against Filippo and Bocca,—but he was nevertheless consistent with his own theology. Moreover, his savage attack on Bocca was made ostensibly before he knew whom he was attacking.

In the deepest sense, therefore, the message of the *Divine Comedy*, so far as it touches the interests and expectations of this world is a jeremiad. Indeed, the predicament in which at the outset the strayed pilgrim Dante finds himself, barred by three ravening beasts from the way of safety is, as the prophet Jeremiah himself declared for Israel, the predicament of the human race. "Wherefore a lion out of the forest shall slay them, and a wolf of the evenings shall spoil them, a leopard shall watch over their cities: every one that goeth out thence shall be torn in pieces: because their transgressions are many, and their backslidings are increased."[129] But Jeremiah's God offers a happy earthly future to his chosen people if they will only amend their ways. "For if ye thoroughly amend your ways and your doings. . . . Then will I cause you to dwell in this place, in the land that I gave to your fathers, for ever and ever.[130] Dante, if we are to take him at his word, offers no such comfort to men, even supposing they should "thoroughly amend their ways and their doings."

[128] *Ib.*, xxxii, 73–123.   [129] *Jer.*, v, 6.
[130] *Ib.*, vii, 5, 7.

Even if millennial living on earth, a true earthly paradise, might once have been possible had mankind not shut its eyes to the light, yet now, he seems to say, it is too late. "We are already in the last age of the world."[131] The promised land for those who "thoroughly amend their ways and their doings" lies beyond this world in the Empyrean. But this comfort is also qualified by Dante's terribly literal logic. If it be true that "many are called, few are chosen," then in the last of the many ages of the world few indeed remain to be chosen. Beatrice's words, as she shows her lover the holy city of the blest, are inevitable:

> Behold our city's circuit, oh, how vast!
> Behold our benches now so full that few
> Are they who are henceforward lacking here.[132]

The end of the whole poem may well be, then, as Dante declares it in his letter to Can Grande, "to remove those living in this life from the state of misery and lead them to the state of felicity,"[133] but for the great majority the hope held out must be a "forlorn hope." Latter-day Christian living is a bitter struggle for survival in heaven, and indeed for the most an ineluctable "race unto death" in hell. It seems an ironic conclusion.

THE SPIRIT OF DANTE'S TEACHING

Dante felt himself to be the prophet of no new gospel. There is a tendency, pictorialized by Carlyle, to represent him as a rebellious spirit. Carlyle emphasizes his spiritual loneliness, his tragic and scornful isolation, his "protest and life-long unsurrendering battle against the world." No doubt there may be truth in this to the mood of the aging exile, long dependent upon the salty bread

---

[131] Banquet, II, xv, 115–6.   [132] Par., xxx, 130–2.
[133] 268–70.

of supercilious aliens. By nature, however, Dante was
far from being a misanthrope or a solitary recluse. On
the contrary, his many and intimate friendships—with
Cavalcanti, Cino, Forese, Casella—the susceptibility to
women for which Boccaccio chides him; his eager interest in politics and rapid rise in office; the very insight
into human motives and passions that vitalizes his poetry, and that itself implies wide and varied acquaintance with men and women—all indicate a sociable and
sympathetic nature. But more than this. The Carlylean
conception of Dante represents him as intellectually rebellious. In fact, however, independent as were Dante's
practical judgments on men and affairs, he professed and
largely realized a humility of mind singular in an age
remarkable for dissidence even to the point of heresy.
The thirteenth century is often called the age of faith.
But for certain temperaments the very danger of dif-
fering from orthodox views gave a stimulus to differ.
Dante was not one of these recalcitrants. Amidst the
babel of argument he was resolutely orthodox. The
Summa of Aquinas was in his time made virtually
authoritative by the Church. It embodied that Christian-
Aristotelianism which Dante called "Catholic opinion."
And in line with it, in all essential matters, Dante's
thought moves docilely. He is content to be its interpreter to the laity. In the Paradise, Beatrice is for him
exactly what the Pope is for the membership of the
Catholic Church. She represents that infallible judgment of spiritual truth which the Pope by right divine
exercises.[134]

In the age-long issue between Church and Empire,
Guelph and Ghibelline, Dante took a position which,
though personally independent, really illustrates the more

[134] Beatrice attributes infallibility to her judgment in Par., vii,
19.

his fundamental conservatism. Conciliatory was the final judgment of his essay on *Monarchy*. Though he argues that the Emperor, no less than the Pope, holds his title directly from God, yet this truth, he declares, "is not to be received in such narrow sense as that the Roman prince is subordinate in naught to the Roman pontiff."[135] Their spheres of sovereignty are distinct, but are related to each other as are their respective ends of mortal, and immortal, felicity. "Mortal felicity is in a certain sense ordained with reference to immortal felicity." "Let Caesar, therefore, observe that reverence to Peter which a first-born son should observe to a father, so that illuminated by the light of paternal grace he may with greater power irradiate the world, over which he is set by him alone who is ruler of all things spiritual and temporal."[136] In the full partisan sense, therefore, Dante was neither Guelph nor Ghibelline, but rather in this world-issue, as in the local alignments of Florentine politics, a party by himself. Cacciaguida in paradise prophetically commends him for breaking with his fellow-exiles of the "White" party:

> ". . . it well beseems
> To make thyself a party by thyself."[137]

The split in this case, however, was due to personal differences, or at most to difference of judgment as to political expediency. Cacciaguida unceremoniously calls the other exiles an "evil senseless company," "all ingrates, all mad and furious."[138] We have reason to suppose that Dante disapproved of their "abortive attempt from Lastra, in concert with the Pistoians, to

[135] *On Mon.*, III, xvi, 129–32. P. H. Wicksteed's translation in *Temple Classics*.
[136] III, xvi, 134–40.   [137] *Par.*, xvii, 68–9.
[138] *Par.*, xvii, 62, 64.

effect an entry into the city" of Florence.[139] There is no reason to suppose that Dante ever disavowed the fundamental principles of the "Whites."

Similarly, in the larger issue of Guelphism and Ghibellinism, he was no waverer or turncoat. As is implied in the last words of his essay on *Monarchy*, he consistently upheld the Guelph view of the primacy of the Church against the extreme Ghibelline denial that the Empire was in any degree subordinate. He violently combated, on the other hand, the extreme Guelph assertion of the right of the Church to interfere in matters purely secular and temporal. Both parties, he argues, are to blame for the evils of the time,[140] but the Church herself, thanks to the fatal "donation of Constantine," which, investing her with temporal interests, tempted her to interfere in temporal affairs,[141] is the greater offender. Dante is explicit as to her guilt:

> Say henceforth that the Church of Rome confounds
>   Two powers in herself, and in the mire
>   Fallen, defiles her burden and herself.[142]

The "donation of Constantine," or investment with temporal power, is the eagle which,

> Perchance with holy and benign intent,

covered the chariot of the Church in the earthly paradise with its plumes, and so started the transformation that ended in such bestial shame.[143] St. Peter exclaims in his angry invective against his degenerate successors:

> "It was not our intention that a part
>   Of the Christian people should sit on the right
>   Of our successors, part upon the left;

[139] Cf. Paget Toynbee: *Dante Alighieri*, London, 1910, p. 90.
[140] Cf. *Par.*, vi, 31–3, 97–111.   [141] Cf. *Hell*, xix, 115–7.
[142] *Purg.*, xvi, 127–9.   [143] *Purg.*, xxxii, 124–60.

Nor that the keys, which had been granted me,
  Become an emblem on a standard borne
  In combat against those who were baptized.[144]

He means of course, that his successors treat Guelphs
as the "sheep," Ghibellines as the "goats,"[145] and that
they make war like any temporal prince.

The whole orthodoxy of Dante's political doctrine lies,
as it were, in an appeal from "Philip drunk to Philip
sober." He whom the Church professed had said: "Render unto Caesar the things that are Caesar's." Dante
figuratively paraphrases the idea. Addressing the priest-
hood, he exclaims:

Ah, folk whose duty is to be devout
  And let the saddle be the seat of Caesar,
  If ye know well what God appoints for you,
Behold how fell this wild beast has become
  For lacking the correction of the spurs,
  Since you upon the bridle have laid hand.[146]

Dante's whole political philosophy might indeed be
summed up in the saying of his favorite St. Paul: "Let
every soul be subject unto the higher powers: for the
powers that be, are ordained of God."[147]

Emphatically then, Dante was no rebel against political authority. On the contrary, his lifelong complaint
was that no emperor arose with a hand strong enough
to enforce his authority. Because Henry VII made at
least an attempt, frustrated by death, Dante through
Beatrice assigned to him one of the few remaining
thrones in paradise.[148] If Dante was a rebel at all, he
was a rebel against rebellion, against all and every form
of anarchy, all social or political unrest. He was a true
disciple of the decidedly conservative Apostle to the
Gentiles.

144 Par., xxvii, 46–51.   145 Cf. Mat., xxv, 38.
146 Purg., vi, 91–6.   147 Romans, xiii, 1.
148 Par., xxx, 133–8.

So in the higher spheres of ethics and religion he
was no less a convinced conformist. There is a fine
saying of his in the *Paradise*, that has led many enthu-
siastic, but overhasty, readers to credit him with a singu-
larly modern sympathy with scepticism as the right mood
of the truth-seeker. Here is the passage:

> Our intellect is never satisfied,
>> I plainly see, unless truth be its light,
>> Outside of which there is no truth extends.
> It rests therein, as in his lair a beast,
>> As soon as it is reached; and it can reach it;
>> If not, then each desire would be in vain.
> On this account there springs up like a shoot,
>> Doubt at the foot of truth, and nature it is
>> That drives us summit-ward from height to height.[149]

A "radical empiricist" of the twentieth century might
well be proud to adopt these words as his platform.
But alas, Dante's immediately following words rudely
break the spell. He continues, applying his premises:

> To me this gives assurance; this bids me,
>> Lady, with reverence to question you
>> Of other truth that is obscure to me.

That word translated, properly enough, as "doubt,"
dubbio, has in the present connection no such connota-
tion of scepticism as we moderns might naturally read
into it. It means for Dante merely the meek questioning of a pupil who has perfect faith in the finality of
his teacher's knowledge. Dante's highest test of truth
is the dogmatic authority of the Church. For him, ultimate truth is not only knowable, but known, and in
principle contained in the *Summa* of Aquinas. In effect,
the doctrine of the *Divine Comedy* is a *summa* of that
Summa. If in any issue there may be divergence of

[149] Par., iv, 124–32.

opinion, it would rest on another accepted Church authority.

Dante was wholly of his time. He was abreast of medieval thinking along its entire line, but he put not one foot beyond it. He was not a path-breaker, but he mapped out so clearly and beautifully the route and position of the spirit of his time that he seems to lead rather than to follow it.

Probably, there is but one other who has so richly assimilated and expressed an epoch. That is Goethe. The *Divine Comedy* and *Faust* irresistibly invite comparison. There are so many points in common; there is such a vast difference in outlook. In each poem there is the same dramatic motive,—salvation of an emperilled soul by the influence of womanly love. The ultimate antithesis lies in the quality of the salvation attained. Dante's pilgrim journeys towards a "quiet heaven," a paradise of perdurable peace, where all desire is stilled in fruition. For him, it is God, not the Fiend, who lies in wait for the neophyte's crucial words—"Moment, abide! thou art so fair." For the modern and romantic Goethe, there is no quiet heaven. The last words of his poem form the motto of it all,—"Upward and on!" Fruition is but the fallowing of the spirit for new and vaster desire. The *summum bonum* is not ended perfection, but endless perfectibility. The book of truth is not, as Dante saw it in the Empyrean, a volume finished and boundup, but a serial, ever "to be continued."[150]

Dante was of his age. But the age itself passed with him. He died in 1321. And in that year Francis Petrarch was already seventeen years of age. Though not, intellectually speaking, to be compared with Dante, Petrarch by the conspiracy of events became precisely that

[150] *Cf.* G. Santayana: *Three Philosophical Poets*, Cambridge (U. S. A.), 1910.

which Dante was not,—a pathbreaker. With full self-consciousness he broke up the unity of Dante's theoretically harmonious world. His very weaknesses and vacillations of spirit bring him the closer to us. He felt, as we, the disquieting *doubt*.

One may, if one likes, minimize Petrarch's originality. One may see in his criticisms and innovations only the dissidence of the thirteenth century continued, and in his enthusiasm for classical antiquity only the more emphatic expression of an ancestor-worship that in Italy had never completely died out. But the fact remains that Petrarch's personality dominated the next age. His words in their message and in their beauty to no small degree fecundated the thinking and directed the writing of the renaissance. In that epoch, Dante, though by no means forgotten by his compatriots, was yet, like Chaucer in Elizabethan England, acclaimed rather as an "old master" than as a living leader. Critics like the elegant Bishop della Casa cavilled at what they called the rustic homeliness of his language and style, his lack of decorum and grace; but between him and the poet-exquisites and philosopher-stylists of the "Golden Age" there was a more fundamental opposition of mood. Whatever the professed beliefs of the renaissance—neo-pagan or reactionary Catholic,—the underlying mood of the time was one of spiritual unrest. The seeds of philosophic, as well as of æsthetic, romanticism were already planted, and sprouting side by side with the assiduously watered shoots of classicism. Dante's humility of mind, his worshipful acceptance of "the powers that be," spiritual and temporal, his setting of fruition above desire, were antipathetic to the age of Lorenzo the Magnificent and Machiavelli, as also to that of Galileo and Giordano Bruno. And again his high seriousness before the grave issues of life and death was a tacit rebuke to the gay levity of an Ariosto or the over-refined punctilios and gallant mysticism of a Bembo or Castiglione. Almost the one man of the renaissance—in Italy or elsewhere—temperamentally capable of appreciating Dante, and who did appreciate him and drink deeply of his wisdom and art, was Michelangelo. Yet even in Michelangelo the contrast of the new spirit is the more plainly visible for his many spiritual affinities with the elder poet. Everywhere in Michelangelo's thought, as in his art, there is restless groping for the uncomprehended, the incomprehensible. Acquiescence, conformity, are impossible to him. For him, Dante's seeming praise of doubt is indeed true in the sense I have denied to be Dante's own. For Michelangelo, we feel that doubt, in the strong sense of the word, does spring up like a shoot at the foot of truth. His poetry, his painting, his sculpture are burdened visibly with the

> weight
> Of all this unintelligible world.

The burden of all Dante's song is the perfect intelligibleness of things.

CHAPTER III

THE ART OF DANTE

CHAPTER III

The Art of Dante

"Give heed at least how beautiful I am."

IF Dante and Goethe differed in respect to man's highest good, they had at least a fundamental artistic conviction in common. In his sonnet on *Nature and Art* Goethe said:

> In self-restriction first reveals himself the master,
> And only law can give us liberty.[1]

Dante's art illustrates the maxim. He would have contemned as haughtily as the spokesman of the French *Pleiade*, the classically nurtured Du Bellay, that facile poet who writes

> By his sole genius, without art or learning.[2]

[1] In der Beschränkung zeigt sich erst der Meister, Und das Gesetz nur kann uns Freiheit geben.

[2] Par le seul naturel, sans art et sans doctrine.

Genius is indeed the gift of God; from God also might come the message, the meaningful inspiration; but it is for the poet to earn by the sweat of his brow perfection in the utterance of the message. In fact, Dante nearly anticipates the renaissance conception of poetry. For Spenser, for instance, "poetry is rather no arte, but a divine gift and heavenly instinct, not to bee gotten by laboure and learning, but adorned with both, and poured into the witte by a certain ἐνθουσιασμός and celestiall inspiration."[3] In his notion of inspiration indeed, Spenser is more fully and consciously a Platonist. To his inspired poet come sudden reminiscences of that intelligible world from which each human soul has descended. Dante, I think, regarded inspiration rather as the voice of a personal and provident God, speaking openly to chosen men, or in dream or vision. For proof he would have appealed to Holy Scripture rather than to pagan philosophy.

> O thou imaginative power, that dost
>   At times so snatch us from the things without
>   One heeds not, though a thousand trumpets sound,
> Who moves thee, if the sense offer thee naught?
>   Light moves thee, which in heaven by itself
>   Takes form, or by His will who sends it down.[4]

But Dante would certainly have agreed with Spenser and the renaissance that the poet, however divinely inspired, must yet bring to his art "laboure and learning." Dante's own toil upon the "sacred poem," he says, as if it were a merit, has made him "lean for many years." Milton's intended compliment to Shakspere for "his native woodnotes wild," Dante would have taken as a slur.

[3] *Shepherd's Calendar*, "October," Argument.
[4] Purg., xvii, 13–8.

Indeed, Dante inclines to the extreme mood of conscious art glorified by Théophile Gautier:

> All things are doubly fair
> If patience fashion them
> And care—
> Verse, enamel, marble, gem.
>
> No idle chains endure:
> Yet, Muse, to walk aright,
> Lace tight
> Thy buskin proud and sure.
>
>   *   *   *   *
>
> Chisel and carve and file
> Till thy vague dream imprint
> Its smile
> On the unyielding flint.[5]

He was by nature subtle-minded, and the native quality was obviously fostered by his scholastic training. He was ingenious also, and rejoiced in the difficult for its own sake. The *Divine Comedy* is a mechanism as elaborately and delicately involved and intercogged as a Geneva watch. Generations of earnest students have failed to exhaust its correspondences and symmetries, cross-references and multiple symbolisms. It is an illuminating fact that he preferred before all French and Provençal poets Arnaut Daniel, a writer modern taste sets below a number of his compeers. Dante's complimentary word is significant. Arnaut was "a better *smith* (*fabbro*) of the mother-tongue."[6] In fact, Arnaut delighted in "hammering out" an intricate verse-pattern of odd conceits. He was a master-juggler in the so-called *trobar clus*, or obscure style of poetry. He preferred, and probably invented, that laborious and cacophonous trifle —the *sestina*. This labored art may not have been Dante's

[5] *L'Art*, translated by George Santayana.
[6] Purg., xxvi, 117.

sole reason for admiring Arnaut, but it certainly made
strong appeal. Dante himself at moments almost forgets
the warning of another maxim of Goethe's,—"Art must
never become mere artistry."[7] Fortunately, his high seriousness of purpose saved Dante from this defect of his
quality.

Essay on Vernacular Eloquence

I. Language and Style

In the early years of the fourteenth century, probably
not long after his exile, Dante began a work, which, had
he completed it, would have enlightened us greatly as to
his theory of literary art. Even as a fragment, the essay is
important. Like the numerous "defences" and "arts of
poetry" of the renaissance, of which indeed it is in some
measure a precursor in type, the essay on *Vernacular
Eloquence* begins by vindicating a reformed Italian language against those who deprecated its fitness for literary
use, and then proceeds to legislate the forms and man-
ners of poetry itself. Of the four books projected, only
the first and a fragment of the second are extant. The
fragmentary work itself was brought into notice by an
anonymous translation—probably by Trissino—in 1529.
The Latin original was first published in Paris in 1577.
Trissino brought forward the essay, because it gave
Dante's sanction to his contention, then hotly debated,
that "the highest form of the language should be called
Italian and not Tuscan."[8]

Dante's argument certainly supported Trissino's thesis.
Before defining what he means by the "noble vernacular," Dante scores roundly, one after another, the rude

[7] Die Kunst darf nie ein Kunststück werden."
[8] *Latin Works of Dante*, Temple Classics Edition, Appen. I,
p. 117.

provincialism of the various local idioms of the peninsula, Tuscan almost as severely as the rest. Certain Tuscan poets indeed—notably Cino of Pistoia and "his friend"— have through genius and learning transcended their native limitations, and achieved a language and style of no mean elevation. It is patent that Cino's friend is Dante himself. But such accomplishment is so far rare. It merely points the way. Like the rest of Dante's writings, therefore, the essay on *Vernacular Eloquence* has a strongly personal background. It not only lays down the principles upon which others should go to work, but also sets forth Dante's own performance as an example and model.

To be worthy of its great mission in life and letters, the Italian language, says Dante, must become "illustrious, cardinal, courtly, and curial." By "illustrious" he means that it must have just such qualities as make men "illustrious." It must have intrinsic virtue; it must by exercise have developed that virtue to the full. The "virtue" of a language is twofold,—expressiveness and euphony. Italian as it is spoken has such virtue in spots. Any particular dialect, however, has but a limited range; and all of them have cacophonous inelegancies. It will be the business of the masters of the art of language to form a vernacular which shall retain as many as possible of the native felicities of the several dialects, and to exclude their inelegancies. Dante does not say so, but we may gather from his own practice that he would have this composite language further enriched by the artist's own coinage.

An "illustrious vernacular," so eclectically developed, may properly, he says, be called "cardinal." It will be *the* Italian language. The existing provincial and local idioms will come to be regarded as mere imperfect variants. Time has justified Dante. The illustrious and cardinal vernacular he prescribed, and in his own writing illustrated, differs less from the language of a Carducci six centuries later than Luther's from Goethe's only three centuries later. We should have to admit many more archaic or obsolete expressions in Shakspere, in spite of his enduring popularity.

The natural centres in which such an illustrious and cardinal speech should be moulded would be, according to Dante, the court and the forum. He would with Edmund Spenser call

> court and royall citadell
> The great schoolmaistresse of all courtesy.[9]

He argued, as did the renaissance, that in that highest of social centres must prevail the best usage, so far as elegance is concerned, as in the high court of law and cabinet of ministers must be found the standard of eloquence. Unhappily, in divided and masterless Italy there existed neither imperial court nor imperial forum. Even in this matter of language Dante is eager to press the imperialist cause. He would have delighted to speak of his illustrious vernacular as "the Emperor's Italian" in the precise sense in which a British writer speaks of "the King's English." In fine, the epithets "courtly and curial" are, strictly speaking, only hypothetically applicable to his illustrious and cardinal vernacular. If Italy had an imperial court, an imperial forum, such a speech would be current in these. Meanwhile, he asserts, "we have a court, though in the body scattered."[10] This is the body of cultivated men of letters, poets, that is, "makers" by divine right of genius of beautiful and eloquent speech. To these Dante therefore appeals, and as one of these justifies his precept and example.

In the making of the new language these artists are

[9] *Fairie Queene*, III, vi, 1.
[10] Vernac. Eloq., I, xviii, 54–5.

not to be left entirely to their own instincts and tastes. Dante felt already and powerfully the spell of classical antiquity,—Roman antiquity especially, since the Greek language was unknown to him and practically so to his age. On the other hand, though he probably did not read Hebrew itself, the Hebraic spirit and style, persistent even in the Vulgate translation of the Bible, greatly affected his style and diction. It is, however, to the Roman Virgil, as will be remembered, that he definitively gives thanks for the fair style that has done him honor.

In Dante's view, Virgil—and the classic writers generally—wrote in what was precisely analogous to Dante's own "illustrious vernacular." They had actually produced what he desired his own countrymen to produce—an eclectic language fused from selected bits of everyday speech, and enriched by the poets' own invention. Classic Latin, as classic Greek, was therefore for him not a natural growth out of popular usage, but a product of conscious and individualistic fine art. Such is his meaning when he declares that "the vernacular followeth use and the Latin art."[11] These artificial and conventional literary languages he calls "grammars" and regards them for their assumed stability and universality as providential concessions to mitigate the curse of the Tower of Babel.

In effect, therefore, Dante was prescribing for Italian just what Virgil and his peers had actually done for Latin. So when he acknowledges Virgil as his master-model, he does not mean, as a renaissance poet might well have meant by a similar acknowledgment, a literal following of the Roman poet's Latin rhetoric. Dante's "illustrious vernacular" is not a Latinized Italian in the sense in which the English of an Ascham or Hooker is a Latinized English. It was rather Virgil's process of re-

[11] Banquet, I, v ,104.

forming the base vernaculars of Augustan Italy that
Dante followed towards the base vernaculars of his own
Italy.

To regard, as Dante thus does, his "illustrious vernacular" as the product of conscious literary fine art, is
almost inevitably to invite a confusion between language
and style. In the first book of the essay on *Vernacular
Eloquence* Dante is clearly prescribing for a possible national language. His "illustrious vernacular" would be
the natural everyday medium of communication between
educated and cultivated people. It would be spoken at
court as soon as ever Italy should come to possess a
court.[12] When, however, in the second book, regarding
the "illustrious vernacular" purely in its applicability to
poetry, he proceeds to the enquiry what themes, forms,
moods of poetry are the ideally best, he unconsciously
shifts his ground. We are now told that only the most
highly gifted poets should presume to employ the "illustrious vernacular," and they only when treating of the
worthiest themes, the gravest and most serious concerns
of life. It should be consecrate to the expression of high
patriotism in the issue of war, of the marriage of true
minds in love, of the zeal of virtue in action. Even so,
there are ways of singing of these themes too in which
the use of the "illustrious vernacular" would be im-
proper. The theme of "arms" may be handled satirically,
that of "love" familiarly or intimately, that of "virtue"
didactically or argumentatively. The less exalted mood
demands a less exalted manner of speech. The most
exalted poetic mood Dante calls the "tragic" mood. For
him, as for the critics of the middle ages generally, the
terms "tragedy" and "comedy" have lost all association
with dramatic form. By "tragic" handling of a theme he
means simply the most grave and serious handling pos-

[12] *Vernac. Eloq.*, I, xviii, 18–20.

sible,—what Spenser means when he exclaims—

> How I could reare the Muse on stately stage,
> And teache her tread aloft in buskin fine.[13]

Spenser does not mean that he could, or would, necessarily write *plays*.

Dante's restrictions of the use in poetry of his "illustrious vernacular" are not yet fully stated. To fit this noblest language there must be provided not only the noblest themes, the noblest attitude of mind towards these noblest themes, but also the noblest poetic form. "If our subject," writes Dante," appears fit to be sung in the tragic style, we must then assume the illustrious vernacular language, and consequently we must bind up a canzone. If, however, it appears fit to be sung in the comic style, sometimes the middle and sometimes the lowly vernacular should be used; and the discernment to be exercised in this case we reserve for treatment in the fourth book. But if our subject appears fit to be sung in the elegiac style, we must adopt the lowly vernacular alone."[14]

Unhappily, the fourth book of the essay was never written, or at least has not come down to us. We are left therefore to guess as best we can at Dante's meaning. It seems manifest, however, that now by "illustrious vernacular" he means a style rather than a language. Roughly speaking, it appears to be what Matthew Arnold intended in his phrase "the grand style in poetry," as by "tragic style" Dante comes close to intending that mood of "high seriousness" which for Arnold marks poetry truly great. By the same token, the distinctions indicated in the terms "middle" and "lowly" vernacular are again primarily aesthetic and stylistic rather than

[13] *Shep. Cal.*, "October," 112–3.
[14] *Vernac. Eloq.*, II, iv, 41–9. Wicksteed's translation.

linguistic. Dante implies as much in his letter to Can Grande, where he remarks that tragedy and comedy differ in their mode of speech, tragedy being exalted and sublime, comedy lax and humble."[15] He is following, as he explicitly states, the authority of Horace; and he agrees with Horace's qualification that upon occasions comedy may assume the tragic elevation and conversely. His own practice in the *Divine Comedy*, furthermore, proves that he quite grasped Horace's true intention. He has, as he tells Can Grande, made the language of his poem "lax and humble," as befitting a comedy.[16] But, on the other hand, he takes full advantage of Horace's concession that upon fit occasion comedy may rise to the exaltation and sublimity of tragedy. In the episode of the Demons,[17] comic in both the technical and the popular sense of the word, Dante's language is "lax and humble," even colloquial and coarse. The manner is carefully conformed to the matter. Again, arriving in his narrative at the uttermost abyss, he protests the incompetency of any speech of man to supply words "harsh and hoarse" enough for the horror of the place, yet with the aid of the Muses he will, he says, do his best to see "that the word and fact be not diverse."[18] So, especially in his rhymes, he chooses the harshest, roughest sounds Italian is capable of,—*chiocce, rocce; abbo, gabbo, babbo; Osteric, Tambernic, cric*; and the like. On the other hand, there are passages in the *Hell* surely as "exalted and sublime" as any in his own "tragic" *canzoni*, in which by his own prescription he must have used the "illustrious vernacular." I mean, of course, the chastely exalted confession of Francesca da Rimini,[19] the heroic narrative of Ulysses,[20] or the tragic horror of

[15] *Epist.*, x, 209–12.   [16] *Ib.*, x, 222–4.
[17] *Hell*, xxi–ii.   [18] *Hell*, xxxii, 1–12.
[19] *Ib.*, v, 88–138.   [20] *Ib.*, xxvi, 90–142.

Ugolino's tale.[21] As for the *Purgatory* and the *Paradise*, it would be hard indeed to find any considerable passage in which the language could in any reasonable sense be called "lax and humble."

Possibly, Dante, like Wordsworth, found his artistic instinct stronger than his theory. Possibly, he came to realize, and quite properly, that although his poem was a comedy in the technical sense that it "beginneth with some adverse circumstances, but its theme hath a happy termination,"[22] yet in its high seriousness it for the most part properly demanded after all the "tragic style." On the other hand, to the statement that its language is "lax and humble," Dante adds an explanatory clause that is very puzzling. The language is "lax and humble," he says, "because it is the vulgar tongue, in which even housewives [*mulierculae*] hold converse."[23] This is curiously ambiguous. It may mean a homely colloquial idiom in contrast to the "illustrious vernacular," or it may mean Italian as opposed to Latin. The latter interpretation would be somewhat supported by the tradition that Dante began his poem in Latin hexameters. Moreover, it is incredible that Dante could seriously maintain that he had made his Francesca da Rimini, or Sapia, or Piccarda, or Beatrice talk like ordinary housewives. Yet, on the other hand, he is in the same passage and in the essay on *Vernacular Eloquence* contrasting the comic with the tragic style, and fitting to the latter, not Latin, but the "illustrious vernacular."

The most probable conclusion would seem to be that, although in the actual use of language no poet was ever more sensitively responsive to shades of fitness, Dante hardly worked out into perfect clarity the theory of the matter. We have seen how in the essay on *Vernacular*

[21] *Ib.*, xxxiii, 4–75.   [22] *Epist.*, x, 203–5.
[23] *Ib.*, x, 224–5.

Eloquence he treats the "illustrious vernacular" first as the national language that is to be, and then as a special poetic diction restricted to the one highest poetic mood and form. Similarly, he wavers in his estimate of any possible vernacular as contrasted with the lordly Latin. In the *New Life*, he almost humorously permits love-poetry to be written in Italian, since the ladies addressed would be unlikely to understand Latin. In the *Banquet*, he waxes eloquent in defence of his mother-tongue, but his avowed reason for using Italian in that commentary on his *canzoni* strikes at least the modern reader as hardly more serious. To write a Latin commentary on Italian poems would be to make the superior serve the inferior. The essay on *Vernacular Eloquence* extends the legitimate scope of the ideal vernacular from the single theme of love to those of "arms" and "virtue." Finally, when Giovanni of Bologna deprecated casting "such weighty themes" as those of the *Divine Comedy* into the "language of the market-place."[24] Dante would justify himself by sending his critic ten cantos of the *Paradise* to read. At the same time, it is one thing to assert the right and duty of an Italian poet to write Italian, another thing to claim for Italian equal worth with Latin. I doubt if Dante would ever have thought of making such a claim.

Though, as I said above, Dante responded sensitively to shades of fitness in style, so that the word and fact might not be diverse, yet he makes little attempt to individualize dialogue. There is indeed the rather naïve realism that puts gibberish into the husky throat of Pluto,[25] and into the brutal mouth of the giant Nimrod,[26] but there is elsewhere almost no mimicry of individual accent. The principal personages of the drama, varied as

[24] *Epist.*, 6–13.   [25] *Hell*, vii, 1.
[26] *Ib.*, xxxi, 67.

are the moods they express, speak the same stately and measured parlance. They are as masks through which the poet speaks his own message. Substantially identical in tone, for instance, are the numerous invectives against Florence, whether spoken by Dante in his own person,[27] or put into the mouth of a Brunetto Latini,[28] or a Forese Donati,[29] or a Cacciaguida,[30] or—as extended to the entire Valdarno—a Guido del Duca.[31]

We need not suppose this prevailing uniformity of dialogue-tone to be due to Dante's dramatic incapacity. The maxim which governed his art no less than teaching was that spoken by the youth in whitest raiment of his New Life,—"Ask not more than is needful for thee."[32] In principle, the maxim rests on the authority of St. Paul,[33] and underlies the Catholic notion of "economy." It was not needful for Dante's purpose that he should individualize his characters more than he does. He is concerned to present not character-studies, but examples of good and evil, and mouthpieces of instruction. Moreover, by choosing always personages familiar to his readers by personal acquaintance or contemporary report, or known in history or legend or literature, he can assume that his readers will do their own individualizing.

So it comes that behind the lifelike and remembered masks he speaks every part, and in his own poet's voice. Behind the flushed face of the stormy St. Peter it is he, victim of the ambitious machinations of Pope Boniface VIII, who fulminates against the abuses of the Papacy; behind the pathetic loveliness of Francesca da Rimini it is he, the poverty-driven exile, who remembers in wretchedness his happy time; behind the

[27] Purg., vi, 127–51.
[28] Hell, xv, 61–78.
[29] Purg., xxiii, 94–111.
[30] Par., xv–xvi.
[31] Purg., xiv, 25–66.
[32] xii, 40–1.
[33] I Cor., xii, 7.

visage, bloody from the new horrible repast, of the grim Ugolino, it is he again, the patriot betrayed by treachery to the "salt bread of others," who metes out infamy to his foes. By a ventriloquism less endurable, he makes other characters—most of all the most gentle Beatrice—speak his schoolmaster's lesson. We have seen how useful, from a purely pedagogical point of view, is Beatrice's lecture on the moon-spots; but what a libel it is on the memory of the Florentine maid who had in her something of that other Beatrice of Shakspere's, born under a dancing star! Did not she too make merry with her companions over the languishing of her lover?[34] And again how incompatible with her tender charity seems it that her last word to her lover in heaven should be, not a solicitude for him, but a curse—even though for a sinner!

ESSAY ON VERNACULAR ELOQUENCE
II. Poetic Forms

It was perhaps also the schoolmaster in Dante that would restrict the "illustrious vernacular" to just one illustrious poetic form. In principle, he thus anticipates the exclusiveness of the renaissance classicists who, to use the disdainful word of the representative Du Bellay, characterized all but a few illustrious forms as mere "spiceries that corrupt the taste of the tongue."[35] Only, whereas the humanist critic would cast aside all medieval poetic forms, except the sonnet, for the classic forms—epigram, elegy, ode, epistle, satire, eclogue, regular comedy and tragedy, epic,—Dante singles for approval three of the medieval and Italian inventions,—canzone, ballata, sonnet. But of these three forms he regards the

[34] New Life, xiv, 50–4.
[35] La Deffence et illustration de la langue francoyse, chap. iv.

canzone as easily supreme. And he gives in his scholas-
tically precise way five reasons for this estimate. First,
the word "canzone" means a "song." The fact that a
particular kind of song should have received the generic
name would indicate that it was more representative
than any other. Secondly, canzoni stand on their own
feet, as it were, whereas ballate, as accompaniments to
dance, require the feet of performers. Thirdly, canzoni
bring the greatest honor to their authors. Fourthly, they
are most "fondly preserved." Fifthly, since "in works of
art, that is noblest which embraces the whole art," so
canzoni, embracing as they do the "whole of the art" of
poetry, must be the noblest.[36]

The most interesting of these five reasons is the last.
It would be more interesting still had Dante explained
just what he meant by the assertion that canzoni contain in themselves the whole of the art of poetry. For
proof, however, he contents himself with what seems a
naïve tautology. "Now," he says, "that the whole of the
art of poetic song is embraced in canzoni is proved by
the fact that whatever is found to belong to the art is
found in them; but the converse is not true." Such a
proof hardly forwards us much. We may infer, however,
his meaning to be that the canzone possesses greater
variety in unity than any other. Dante himself in the
second book abundantly illustrates the complexity of its
metrical organism. We need not discuss that here, therefore.

Dante's preferment of the canzone is not without analogy in principle to Edgar Allan Poe's analysis of the
ideal poetic form in his famous study of the Raven.
The normal canzone about measures up to the ideal
length prescribed by Poe; and Poe also prided himself
upon having utilized the maximum of metrical effects

[36] Vernac. Eloq., II, iii.

in his poem. He might not have claimed that it embraced the whole of poetic art, but certainly that it embraced an unusual proportion.

That Dante should hold the *canzone* form so highly is not at all surprising. He had mental traits in common with Poe. As I have already noted, his highly subtle and ingenious mind delighted in difficult technical problems in artistry no less than in theology. And the *canzone*-form, fully exploited, is certainly as difficult as any poetic form ever devised,—as any, at least, that is not mere trickery in rhyme. For the structure of the *canzone* is logical and beautiful as well as difficult.

It has puzzled some critics that after declaring the *canzone* the supreme poetic form, Dante should compose his masterpiece, the *Divine Comedy*, in the relatively simple *terza rima*, which in the essay on *Vernacular Eloquence* he would seemingly have classed among "other illegitimate and irregular forms of poetry." The suggestion has been made, accordingly, that the breaking off of the essay might have been due to a "revolution in Dante's ideas as to the scope of poetry in the vulgar tongue wrought by his conception of the *Divine Comedy*."[37]

This conclusion rests on two counts. It is argued that, whereas the essay declares the vulgar tongue competent to treat the themes of "arms, love, and virtue," the *Divine Comedy* discusses also the still higher theme of religion. Secondly, it would seem to be absurd that the poet should class the greatest achievement of his genius among "illegitimate and irregular forms of poetry."

As to the first count, Dante expressly declares to Can Grande that the purpose of the *Comedy* is to instil the idea of virtue. He writes: "But the branch of philosophy which regulates the work in its whole and in its

[37] P. H. Wicksteed in *Temple Classics* Edition, p. 120.

parts, is morals or ethics, because the whole was un-
dertaken not for speculation but for practical results."[38]
Dante, I think, consistently lives up to this declaration.
As not infrequently, the confusion is not in his mind,
but in that of his critics. The high mysteries of the
Catholic faith are, it is true, expounded in the *Paradise*, but neither "for speculation" nor in a speculative
mood. They are merely stated *ex cathedra* as the sanction for Christian ethics, for the conforming of human
"desire and will" to

> The Love that moves the sun and other stars.

Dante might well hold the vulgar tongue competent to
declare to the laity the grand conclusions of Catholic
theology, but not adequately to debate the subtile arguments and fine distinctions on which it rests. In other
words, Dante in the *Divine Comedy* has no thought of
proving the faith. Such enterprise would be for him,
layman and vernacular poet, a piece of presumptuous
supererogation.

> Ye have the Old and the New Testament,
>   And of the Church the Shepherd is your guide;
>   For your salvation deem ye this enough.[39]

This warning of Beatrice Dante has taken unreservedly
to heart. He would but shape in beauty an image of
truth, submissively received, such that unlearned men
might lovingly worship. Even though they might fail of
full understanding of that truth, he would yet have it
say to them:

> Give heed at least how beautiful I am.

As to the second count, it is hardly accurate to say
that Dante classed his masterpiece among "illegitimate

---

[38] *Epist.*, x, 271–5.   [39] *Par.*, v, 76–8.

and irregular forms of poetry." So to describe the marvelous architectonic of the *Divine Comedy*, so majestic in the whole design, so exquisitely proportioned and interrelated in all its parts, would indeed be a case of overweening modesty. It must be remembered, however, that this structural magnificence is impressed on the form by the matter. Stripped of Dante's unique meaning, the structure of the *Comedy* crumbles. Another poet could not use the emptied shell to fill with new meat, as one might pour a new content into the empty *schema* of a *canzone* or a sonnet. Thus Dante employed, for instance, a scale of certain symbolic numbers for the proportioning of his poetic edifice,—three and ten, and also ten distributed into its component one, two, and seven. The meaning of these symbolic divisions has been explained in the last chapter. Now obviously, apart from that meaning, a structural plan so based would be merely capricious. In the *canzone*-form, on the contrary, there is, as Dante meticulously illustrates in the second book of his essay, a right numerical proportion, irrespective of the content and determinable *a priori*, for all its parts,—syllables in the foot, feet in the line, lines and rhymes and divisions in the stanza, stanzas in the whole. It is a ready-made metrical organism.

Comparatively speaking, certainly, *terza rima* is, in the sense Dante undoubtedly intended, a poetic form—if form it may be called—"illegitimate and irregular." It observes a certain principle of continuance in the cross-linking of rhymes, but that is all. It is bound up into no recognized whole, and therefore can have no regularly functional parts. One continues the ternary sequence *ad libitum*. No doubt, an organic structure might be given to *terza rima*,—as actually by Shelley in his *Ode to the West Wind*. But in Dante's day, none such was recognized.

I can see no reason, therefore, for inferring a revolutionary change of mind on Dante's part. He may well have continued to regard terza rima as "illegitimate and irregular" for possessing no inner law or principle which should build it up into an organic and normal whole. He may well have continued to prefer before all others the set and artificial, but rich and beautiful, form of the canzone. Indeed, he shows his abiding joy in his own canzoni by citing them several times in the Divine Comedy itself. One of the ingenuously delightful self-compliments in literature is Dante's account of how he and Virgil and all the eager spirits at the base of the mount of purgatory lingered to hear Casella sing one of Dante's own canzoni, and how the stern Cato rebuked them for delaying, and how Virgil, abashed by the rebuke, lent to his feet "that haste which mars the dignity of every act."[40] We are bound to feel that a rare poem indeed which could make Virgil, "l'altissimo poeta" and heaven-sent guide, so far forget his responsibility and himself. One would give much to know whether Dante wrote the passage—as some others—with or without a smile.

Dante's Canzoni and Other Lyrics

I am not sure that modern taste responds quite so absorbedly to Dante's canzoni. They are—most of them—highly intellectualized poems, subtle, allusive, remote. Beyond all cavil, they contain nobly moving passages. To call them sweetly musical is to say little. How difficult is it for Italian verse to be otherwise! But as wholes, they are, I venture to think, difficult in the reading and a little intangible in the effect. One misses, except at rare moments, the tender and ardent humanity of Petrarch

[40] Purg., ii, 106–iii, 11.

at his best. There still clings about Dante's expression of sentiment something of the fastidiously conventional elegance of the troubadour, about his expression of thought something of the argumentative subtlety of the schoolman. No doubt there is much of this argumentative mood in the *Divine Comedy* also. It is a descent towards the mood of prose even there; but there it is given at least dramatic fitness. An argumentative lyric is almost a contradiction in terms. Guido Guinicelli's famous *canzone* on "the gentle heart" is philosophical, but its tone is not argumentative; its abstract ideas are warmed into vital images and dramatic suggestions. Dante's closely correspondent *canzone*—that which heads the fourth book of the *Banquet*—is rather, like Pope's *Essay on Man*, a rhymed disquisition.

The most vivid of Dante's *canzoni*, the one that bites most deeply into the modern imagination, is the one beginning—

As harsh in my discourse would I fain be.[41]

It is not, any more than the *Hell*, an altogether pleasant poem; it contains not a few frigid conceits and troubadour conventionalities; but it is passionately real. In its hard and wiry lines we hear no longer the philosophic *conoscente*, the adept of a somewhat languorously "sweet style," but a man whose desire is stronger than himself, and is turned all bitter by the thwarting. Probably, as has been said, the stony-hearted object of his desire is the Gentucca mysteriously named by Bonagiunta in purgatory. Dante may have met her while at Lucca in the June of 1314. If so, he must have composed the *canzone* just after completing the *Hell*. His speech is as if still crisped by the fires of the abyss. He cries out upon the stony-hearted one:

[41] *Canz.*, xii in Moore's edition of the *Opere*.

> Oh me, that she howls not
> For me, as I for her in the hot caldron![42]

This is indeed a new style, but not altogether a "sweet new style." It is far away enough from that earlier decorous idealization of the Compassionate Lady or his later well-nigh impersonal worship of the Lady Beatrice. Certainly, it arrests and startles. Startling again is it to hear the once so gentle poet long to clutch the fair tresses, his lash and scourge, and from tierce to vesper and evening bells to hold her fast—not compassionately nor courteously, but like a bear taking his sport, and to gaze the while deep, deep into her eyes; and then at last, avenged, to render her peace with love.

The accent of a passion almost brutal in its violence, the sudden gracefully tender turn, are of the manner of things that, in Ben Jonson's opinion, made John Donne "the first poet of the world." Nowhere else is Dante so modern, so romantic. One is reminded of John Keats's advice to the melancholy lover—

> Or if thy mistress some rich anger shows,
> Emprison her soft hand, and let her rave,
> And feed deep, deep upon her peerless eyes.[43]

Only, of course, Keats's lines lack altogether the virility of Dante's.

Dante's other lyrical pieces—his *sestine*, *ballate*, sonnets—are in their degree much like the *canzoni* in mood and mode. Love is the common theme of nearly all, but they are—most of them—more compact with thought than with passion, rather pithy than poignant. Yet the high devotional mood of love has never found lovelier lyric expression than in the last sonnet of the *New Life*. Few poems of love in lighter vein are more daintily exquisite than the sonnet to Guido Cavalcanti, telling how

[42] ll. 59–60. Wicksteed's translation.
[43] *Ode on Melancholy*.

Dante wishes that he and Guido and Lapo Gianni might be wafted in an enchanted ship on a tranquil ocean in loving converse with their three ladies forever.

To express the virtue of Dante's lyric poetry there naturally springs to one's lips his own favorite epithet— noble. Nobility of sentiment conjoined with nobility of style and music is the prevailing characteristic of his song. It is almost without setting or imagery. He draws for us postures of the spirit, colorless, but sharply and exactly outlined. I have called his genre noble; it is noble also in the narrower sense of aristocratic. It is the poetry of an inner circle, of the select few. Dante was a Platonist in more than his idealization of love and beauty. Though he appears to have read nothing of Plato's writings except part of the *Timaeus* in translation, he could find much of Plato's outlook in St. Augustine and other Christian writers. And Dante's temper was strangely like Plato's. Dante had the same intense intellectualism touched with imaginative sensibility, the same sympathetic responsiveness to manifold humanity checked by a fastidiousness, at once instinctive and reasoned, that made him disdainful of all but the best in whatever kind. He calls himself through Virgil's mouth a "disdainful soul."[44] Boccaccio uses the same words.[45] And Dante's "first friend," Guido Cavalcanti, expresses himself as no less astonished than grieved that for political preferment or whatever reason, Dante should stoop from his noble exclusiveness, to consort with the vulgar herd. Cavalcanti protested in a famous sonnet,[46] which

[44] *Hell*, viii, 44.   [45] *Life of Dante*, chap. xii.
[46] *Io vengo il giorno a te infinite volte.* The occasion of the rebuke is not positively known. A plausible guess is that Guido intended Dante's entering actively into politics, and in the party of the "Whites," the bourgeois party led by the parvenu Vieri de' Cerchi. *Cf.* E. Lamma, in *Questioni Dantesche*, Bologna, 1902.

remains one of the most interesting, if in its occasion puzzling, contemporary documents concerning Dante. I therefore translate it in full.

> I come to thee infinite times a day
>> And find thee thinking too unworthily:
>> Then for thy gentle mind it grieveth me,
>> And for thy talents all thus thrown away.
> To flee the vulgar herd was once thy way,
>> To bar the many from thine amity;
>> Of me thou spakest then most cordially
>> When thou hadst set thy verse in right array.[47]
> But now I dare not, so thy life is base,
>> Make manifest that I approve thine art,
>> Nor come to thee so thou mayst see my face.
> Yet if this sonnet thou wilt take to heart,
>> The perverse spirit leading thee this chase
>> Out of thy soul polluted shall depart.

Anyone accusing Dante Alighieri of undignified gregariousness must indeed have been himself exclusive. And exclusive Cavalcanti was intellectually and aesthetically as well as politically and socially. He has even been credited with a philosophy borrowed from the Arabian Avempace, advocating absolute internment of oneself in oneself, "the world forgetting, by the world forgot."[48] It cannot be doubted that Cavalcanti increased the young Dante's bias towards an aristocratic envisagement of life and art. Cavalcanti protests haughtily in his metaphysical canzone on Love:

Adept[49] I ask unto this task of mine.

[47] I. e., in the New Life, in which Dante had spoken of Guido as his "first friend." The book was also apparently dedicated to him.

[48] Cf. G. Salvadori: La poesia giovanile e la canzoni d'amore di Guido Cavalcanti, Rome, 1895.

[49] Conoscente. Donna mi prega, l. 5.

And he dismisses the poem:

> Ode, thou mayst go thy ways, unfaltering,
> Where pleaseth thee: I have thee so adorned
> That never scorned shall be thy reasoning
> By such as bring to thee intelligence:
> To bide with others mak'st thou no pretence.

Dante caught the accent and in his lyric emphasized it
again and again. Citizen of democratic Florence as he
was, his earlier poetic appeal was as exclusive and aristocratic as that of his Provençal masters, on the one
hand, or, on the other hand, as that of the most courtly
Platonizers of the renaissance.

THE DIVINE COMEDY

The mood and manner of his narrative masterpiece,
the *Divine Comedy*, are of course in the high sense of
the word as noble as his noblest lyric. The appeal of the
Comedy, on the other hand, is professedly not aristocratic,—not exclusive but universal. By Dante's canons
of art, the genre of comedy involved a more "lax and
humble" style, a more popular utterance. Moreover, as
Dante wrote Can Grande, the moving purpose of his
work was "to remove those living in this life from the
state of misery and lead them to the state of felicity."[50]
And the two essential ingredients in the prescription of
the Healer were humility and love. He perhaps might
have replied to Cavalcanti that he stooped to the "vulgar herd" only to save it. Dante belonged, however, to
the wing of medieval philosophical opinion that made
understanding antecedent to emotion. We must know
God before we can love him, and we love him only in
the degree of our knowledge. What Dante says of the

[50] *Epist.*, x, 266–70.

blessedness of the angels is true as well of human blessedness.

> And thou shouldst know that the delight of all
>   Is as their vision's fathoming of truth,
>   Wherein the intellect of all finds rest.
> By this is to be seen how blessedness
>   Is founded on the act which sees, and not
>   On that which loves, which follows afterwards;
> And of this sight the measure is desert,
>   Which is brought forth by grace and by goodwill;
>   And such is the advance from grade to grade.[51]

If understanding is according to desert, desert must be in
the measure of understanding. When, therefore, Dante
addresses himself to those "who have sound intellects,"[52]
he meant by implication those who are capable of salvation. He believed, as we have seen, that but relatively
few such remained to be considered. Only with moral
and intellectual aristocrats is he concerned. To receive his
message, the reader's heart and mind must be "gentle."

> The sun strikes full upon the mud all day:
>   It remains vile, nor the sun's worth is less.[53]

This doctrine of the correlation of grades of intelligence with grades of reward appears to be reflected in
the art of the Comedy. In the Hell Dante writes as if
for a lower intelligence than he demands for the Purgatory, and he warns away all but the intellectually elect
from the Paradise. Surely, understanding of evil is no
easier than understanding of good; but Dante seems to be
applying his doctrine of "accommodation" to aesthetic
ends. "In church with saints, and with guzzlers in the
tavern," he exclaims with half humorous deprecation of
the diabolic escort provided for Virgil and himself in the

[51] Par., xxviii, 106–14.   [52] Hell, ix, 61.
[53] Guinicelli: Of the Gentle Heart, ll. 31–2.

circle of the Barrators.[54] He must accommodate himself to circumstances. So, generally, he adapts his mood and style, and to a certain extent even his personal sympathy, to each otherworld kingdom in turn. I have already referred to the resultant scaling of conversational values. More broadly speaking, the *Hell* appeals to humanly concrete and personal interests. We are in the realm of materiality.

There is indeed good reason for the greater human interest of the *Hell*. There is richer material for the dramatic artist. The "lost folk" may be a sad lot, but they are psychologically more interesting than the satisfied saints and the lachrymose penitents. This is no cynical comment. There is sound psychological reason,—one that Milton also illustrates in his interesting Satan. For Dante, the redeemed are actuated by one sole impulse,— meek love. They may express their love with greater or less intensity, but they have lost all complexity of character, all conflict of motives, nearly all individuality. Their personalities, as well as their persons, fade away in the glory that swathes them. The damned remain intensely, if unpleasantly, human. Indeed, it is a kind of hypocrisy to call many of them unpleasant at all. Who thinks of her sin when listening to the tenderly beautiful words of Francesca, or is not moved to admiration by the magnificence of Farinata,

> upright with breast and countenance,
> As if he entertained great scorn of hell?[55]

Who is not touched by the fatherly solicitude of the elder Cavalcanti, in the midst of his torment anxiously enquiring after his son,[56] or by the sad dignity of Brunetto Latini, still wise and helpful in his shame?[57]

[54] *Hell*, xxii, 14–5.
[55] *Hell*, x, 25–6. Wicksteed's translation.
[56] *Hell*, x, 58–72.   [57] *Ib.*, xv.

Certainly not Dante himself, who swooned for pity of Francesca, and went with bent head beside Brunetto, "as one who walks in reverence." What matters that the indomitable Ulysses is met among the evil counsellors, when he tells how bravely he and his age-weary men followed their quest of "virtue and knowledge" in that last voyage? By such dauntlessness, we feel, is puny man raised above the easy-going gods. Again, how Count Ugolino rises above his grisly tale, a figure of Aeschylean grandeur! And I say nothing of the sad, uncomplaining nobility of Virgil himself, damned for unfealty to a Lord he never knew. Even where our moral sympathies are not engaged, we can yet understand and respond to these lively sinners, in so many respects so like ourselves. We enjoy the harlequin cunning of the Navarrese barrator, as he turns the tables on his fiendish tormentors.[58] We are half amused, half sorry, to have the wily Guido of Montefeltro outwiled by the Pope.[59] We feel it almost priggish in Virgil to rebuke Dante for listening to the squabble between Master Adam and Sinon.[60] Aristophanes or Lucian never invented a situation more divertingly incongruous than this debate in hell between the Greek spy and the Tuscan counterfeiter as to which was the wickeder. We instinctively side with the hapless Bocca degli Abbati against Dante, who might at least have apologized for accidentally kicking him in the face: and, considering Bocca's defenceless condition, frozen neck-deep in ice, we feel it hardly chivalrous for Dante to tear out his hair by the handful.[61] No doubt the wretch was obstinate in refusing to disclose his identity, but the shame that restrained him was after all rather commendable for one in hell.

All the dramatist in Dante responds to this mani-

[58] *Ib.*, xxii.
[60] *Hell*, xxx.
[59] *Ib.*, xxvii.
[61] *Ib.*, xxxii.

fold variety of type and mood and motive. As a good Catholic he has no business to be sympathetic with the damned. But in vain Virgil rebukes him for his inquisitive interest. Perhaps Dante would indicate that his spiritual fastidiousness was dulled by the gross vapors of the subterranean abyss, "with the guzzlers in the tavern." With the earth-imprisoned ones his own imagination is earthly, bound to sense-imagery, to concrete fact. In the last chapter I have discussed the edifying symbolism involved in the picture much as the lines of a fortress have been implied in the seemingly innocent landscape-sketch of a military spy. The reader of the *Hell* may easily ignore the hidden edification, and enjoy the variegated and peopled landscape.

In suiting his style to the hard and grim reality of hell, Dante was far from eliminating from his first canticle all beauty. I have already referred to the loveliness or nobility of such characterizations as those of Francesca da Rimini and Ulysses. Such occasional beauty is vastly heightened by the grisliness and squalor against which it is drawn. An effect worthy of Rembrandt, for instance, is the sudden glory of the angelic messenger against the flame-shot murk of the City of Dis. The angel looms majestic in his haughty and scornful isolation. The angels of purgatory are more benign, but less magnificent; and in paradise, "staled by frequence," they are even less impressive than the human blest.

There is a popular, almost childlike side to the *Hell.* In the grisly-grotesque humor of the episode of the demons[62] Dante appeals to the popular audience that shook its sides at the antics of the devils at hell-mouth in the religious plays presented in the public squares.

O thou who readest, thou shalt hear new sport,

[62] *Hell,* xxi–xxii.

he promises. Adapted to the same taste are Minos with his convenient "index" tail, and the other infernal monsters. Antique Charon with the flame-ringed eyes and woolly beard, three-headed Cerberus, the Minotaur, Pluto and the giant Nimrod with their savage gibberish, the stern Centaurs, the half-dragon Geryon,—all these are drawn from classical legend, but deformed into grotesque caricature by the medieval imagination. Dante's Satan again is more the ogre of a fairy-tale than Milton's tragic rebel, majestic even in his downfall. Gigantic, hairy, inexpressive, flapping his bat-wings, mumbling a writhen victim in each of his three bestial mouths,—such an arch-fiend is but the nightmare of a childlike fancy. He lacks altogether the tragic spirit, which even Goethe's Mephistofeles shows in that moment when, throwing off the mask of cynical buffoonery, he turns on Faust with the haughty, bitter might of a prince of hell.

There are two moments of spiritually poignant tragedy in the Hell. Francesca da Rimini and Count Ugolino confess their sin. They are uncomplaining in their everlasting torment. But their very confessions prove their constancy, even nobility, of character. There lies the tragic pity of it. Even if we repudiate as a lying metaphysical nightmare the notion of eternal damnation, we cannot deny the nemesis that waits on sin. Whether the avenging god strikes from his heaven or from within our own breasts, he strikes. And in the agony of Francesca and Ugolino, as in that of Oedipus or Orestes, we are made to feel and dread his might overwhelmingly. The case of Ulysses in the Hell is different. Ulysses makes no confession of guilt. He is damned for evil counsel, but we hardly take the charge seriously. The crafty deeds imputed against him seem but fair stratagems of war. There is no element of moral tragedy in his tale. His purpose was high. He was defeated, not by his own weakness, but by the hostile forces of nature, or the jealous gods.

The horror of nearly all the rest of the *Hell* is physical. We are shown unhappy wretches blown headlong on the storm, sprawled sodden under pestilential rain or snow, buried in filthy bogs or more filthy dung, swimming in torrents of blood or molten pitch, pelted by fire or prisoned in ice, metamorphosed into poisonous trees or serpents, planted head down in burning pits, hideously maimed and loathsomely diseased. We hear a continual din of groaning and weeping, reviling and blaspheming, above the hissing and roaring of the infernal elements. Stenches unendurable are suggested,—of sulphurous blasts and stagnant waters, of diseased blood and putrid sores and human excrement. All is in restless flux. The sinners are forever running or writhing, and mauling and biting and maiming one another. Yet strange to say, when addressed by Dante, they answer calmly and talk informingly—often of impersonal matters. For Dante's edification—and ours—they become wondrous stoics.

There is certainly something almost childish in the long catalogue of loathsomeness. But Dante's audience was trained to expect it. Preachers, poets, painters, sculptors had for generations vied with one another to make hell more hellish, the divine justice more intolerable. It is Dante's style and the architecture of his poem, his art rather than his invention, that raises him above the rest. Indeed, his ingenuity in horror at times almost defeats his purpose. The shoving contest of the avaricious against the prodigal has an almost comic suggestion of modern "push-ball." The naked legs of the upsidedown simonists, wiggling in the air, are hardly to be visualized without a smile. The personage who carries his severed head like a lantern, and lifts it up in order that the speaking lips may be more audible, is hardly, I think, awe-inspiring to an adult.

But—"with guzzlers in the tavern." In the Hell, Dante
is retelling an oft-told tale to the popular ear. He is content for the most part to mould his narrative out of the
usual stuff. Those of his hearers who have "sound intellects" may indeed look through the letter to the deeper
truths beneath. But except for the eleventh canto, so different in its doctrinal abstractness from all the rest that
its authenticity has been seriously though unconvincingly
questioned, he does not obtrude his lesson. Like the par-
ish-priest, he would merely horrify his hearers into repentance.

In the Purgatory we rise into an atmosphere less morally repugnant to modern feeling.

> To run o'er better waters now hoists sail
>   The little vessel of my genius as
>   She leaves behind her such a cruel sea.

But it is not merely that the infernal sea is cruel. Because
it is wantonly and futilely cruel we sicken, traversing it.
These craftily contrived and carefully modulated torments, forever unmitigated, rather to be increased after
the day of judgment when the suffering shades shall receive the accursed gift of a more sensitive carnal body,
seem to us the atrocities of an insane devil. We can but
pity the perversion of a noble mind, that having conceived the ineffable sorrow of Francesca, could yet worship in love the personal divinity that should set upon so
sweet and redeemable a soul an eternity of woe.

Dante presented hell as he received it from the theolo-
gians. The ugly cast of it was too set for him to alter
without conscious doctrinal error. The notion of purgatory was still comparatively plastic. He accepted, as we
have seen, substantially the conclusions of Aquinas in
regard to the need and nature of purgation after death.
And, as we have seen also, the scheme underlying is

somewhat mechanistic. Belacqua, hugging his lazy knees
at the base of the Mount like the very brother of Sloth,
strikes us as a queer kind of penitent. If he was in the
end to be permitted self-purification, why in reason hold
back his good will from present performance? Considered as a forfeit, the postponement would be trivial.
What is thrice a human lifetime to eternity? As for the
pains and penalties of purgatory in general, it seems an
all too Hebraic God that should weigh out so nicely his
punitive pound of flesh!

But there is another aspect to the case. Once admitted
to purgatory, the penitents are indeed assured of ultimate
salvation. In addressing certain of them, Dante recog-
nizes this spiritual security:

> O souls, assured to have,
> Whenever it may be, a state of peace. . . .[63]

Immune from the capacity to sin, they are incapable of
new virtue,—so far as virtue is simply the overcoming
of temptation. Between them and perfect peace of mind,
however, is the sense of a debt unpaid. They owe God
more or less penance.[64] Regardless of the fact that God
exacts payment, for them it is a debt of honor; and they
are eager, as men of honor, to satisfy it. Antonio is un-
willing to repudiate an obligation—even to a Shylock.

Dante, moreover, throws over the transaction a poetic
glamor. His penitents pay their "scot of tears" without
questioning its reasonableness. They have learned, as
Dante piously recommends,[65] to abide content with
things as they are. They bless the hand that smites them,
and so go joyously cleansing themselves to appear fair
before their Maker.[66] Theirs is the spirit of the bride
adorning herself for the bridegroom.

[63] *Purg.*, xxvi, 53–4.   [64] *Cf. Ib.*, xi, 70–2; xxiii, 24–5.
[65] Be then content, mankind, with "So it is." *Purg.*, iii, 37.
[66] *Ib.*, xvi, 31–2.

Possibly, there is a touch of "pathetic fallacy" in this conception of purgatory. The poet has a little softened the theologian. Certainly, the emphasis of Aquinas is different,—and it is all very much a matter of emphasis. But the emotional difference, the difference to art, is enormous. The actual torments of purgatory are hardly less grotesque and repellent than those of hell. We meet with figures agonizingly bent double under huge burdens of stone, or movelessly prostrate, nose to earth, or skeleton-like, starved and famishing beside luscious fruit-trees and sparkling springs, or madly racing nowhither, or walking upright in flames. Others we see in hair-cloth, their eyelids locked with sutures of sharp wire, and still others blinded and choking in a black and bitter smoke. But it is not, as in the *Hell*, their anguish, but their consolation, that is emphasized for us.

> I would not, reader, that thou be dismayed
>> From any purpose good, because thou hearest
>> How God wills that indebtedness be paid.
> Give no attention to the form of pain;
>> Think of what follows; think, that at the worst,
>> Beyond the Judgment-Day it cannot go.[67]

This is a little like encouraging a child to swallow a nasty dose. In reality, however, Dante himself pays the slightest possible attention to the form of pain in his *Purgatory*. The prevailing mood of the canticle is not of suffering, even medicinal suffering, but of human friendliness. The major episodes are of warm-hearted reunions and meetings,—of Dante with Casella, Forese and Guinicelli, and of Virgil with Sordello and Statius. Nowhere is Dante so genial, almost playful, as when he tells how Virgil for modesty would hide his identity from the worshipful Statius, and is betrayed to homage by Dante's involuntary

[67] *Purg.*, x, 106–11.

smile.[68] Finally, to crown all, comes Dante's reunion
with Beatrice in an earthly paradise so made doubly
paradise for him.

With this prevailing spirit of friendliness goes also an
atmosphere of cheer and vivacity. Rugged as the way is,
the stars shine on it by night, the sun by day. The air is
full of singing voices. And the interests of earth are far
from forgotten. Dante's converse with the shades is on
letters and art and science as well as morals. They, no
less than he, are ready with bitter invective against the
malice or bungling of earthly states and potentates. They
are eager for the latest news.

To apply a phrase of Charles Lamb's— though doubtless not precisely in his sense,— the *Purgatory* is fitly
a sphere of "middle emotions" between the grim ironies
of the *Hell* and the rarefied ecstasies of the *Paradise*.
Its style also is fitly a mean between the homely and
trenchant vernacular of the more realistic portions of the
Hell and the exalted and stately manner of the *Paradise*.
I doubt not that Dante purposely illustrated herein that
distinction for poetry of noble, middle, and base vernacular alluded to at the beginning of this chapter.

The human qualities of friendliness and cheer lighten
the long toil up the arduous Mount. The talk by the way
is of human interests, human conduct. Even at the top,
in the blissfulness of the recovered Eden, the meeting of
the lover with his reproachful lady is very human in its
lights and shades of rebuke and shame, of forgiveness
and joy. Perhaps in her interpretation for Dante of the
apocalyptic vision of the history of church and state,
which follows their reconciliation, she grows a little stiff
and hieratic. In her rôle of priestess of the mysteries the
woman slips over into the symbol. But at the end, a touch
of almost girlish malice redeems her. She has reminded

[68] *Purg.*, xxi.

Dante once again of his errancy. He innocently replies:

> "I remember not
> That I ever estranged myself from you,
> Nor am I conscious of remorse for it."
> "And if thou canst not bring it to thy mind,"
> She answered with a smile, "remember now
> It was this very day that thou didst drink
> Of Lethe. . . ."[69]

In the trippingly colloquial Italian, the retort is even more vivacious, and in it we hear again for nearly the last time the gay Florentine girl who made merry with her companions over Dante's wan worship of her. In the *Paradise*, she, even more than Dante himself, is "transhumanized," become in her glorified perfection all too edifyingly

> good
> For human nature's daily food.

We feel that she is painfully right when she says—

> "If I should smile, thou wouldst become
> What Semele became, to ashes turned."[70]

Three times only in the *Paradise* does Beatrice appear again quite the woman,—once, when with a flash of humor, she coughs at Dante's touch of family pride in the manner of his greeting of his illustrious ancestor Cacciaguida;[71] and twice over, in her winsome deprecation of his too personal homage—

> "Turn thou and listen, for
> Not only in my eyes is Paradise"—[72]

and—

> "Why with my face art thou enamored so
> As not to turn to that fair garden, which
> Beneath the rays of Christ is blossoming?"[73]

[69] Purg., xxxiii, 91–7.
[70] Par., xxi, 5–6.
[71] Par., xvi, 1–15.
[72] Ib., xviii, 20–1.
[73] Ib., xxiii, 70–2.

For the rest, Dante's words of her are often touchingly
beautiful, but her own words are solemnly didactic or
corrective. While we listen to her speaking, we see her
face under the white veil turn staid and nun-like, the
brows knit with dry reasoning. We hear the sweet voice
harden into argumentative and dogmatic emphasis. Alas,
we feel indeed that no longer in her eyes is paradise.
Our thoughts go back to the schoolroom of our child-
hood. Just such solemnly benevolent eyes—though beam-
ing from behind spectacles, just such a voice—delicately
balanced between encouragement and reproof, had the
gentle spinster who fed us also—however sparingly—of the
"food of angels," and to whose motherliness we turned
in our childish troubles—even as Dante to Beatrice.

> Oppressed with my amazement, to my guide
> I turned me, as a child runs always back
> Thither where he has greatest confidence;
> And she was like a mother who gives help
> At once to her pale, breathless son with voice
> That has been wont to comfort him. . . .[74]

I speak not in a spirit of levity, but with genuine
regret,—not, of course, regret for Beatrice's instinctive
motherliness. Every true maid is something of a mother
to the man she loves. But it is matter for infinite regret,
I feel, that the artist who made Francesca live, and Piccarda, and the young Beatrice, should so cloud his poet's
vision as to see his sweet lady at the last but as a glorified scholastic doctor. It is not that she teaches Dante
her truth. Piccarda also teaches deepest truth, when she
exclaims in her tender humility,—"And His will is our
peace." Her words, simple and calm and beautiful, are
in character, and reveal her character. Her wisdom has
been won by love out of adversity, when the men "more

[74] Par., xxii, 1–6.

used to ill than good" tore her, the young virgin sister, from her sacred retreat, and made of her life then what God knows.[75] If Dante had only treated the emparadised Beatrice with like delicacy and dramatic propriety! If nuns must have been the spokeswomen of the heaven of the Moon, why instead of Beatrice, could not some learned Lady Superior, the great Constance herself, have given that lecture on the spottiness of the planet? But Dante wanted symbolized Theology's authority, and sacrificed Beatrice.

To my thinking, this pedanticizing of Beatrice is the "spot on the sun" of the *Paradise*. In it, the theologian has shouldered out the poet.

Dante, who in the *Hell* had appealed so frankly to the popular ear, austerely warns off from the *Paradise* all but an elect few.

> O ye, who in a very little bark,
>   Eager to listen, have been following
>   Behind my ship that singing makes its way,
> Turn back to look again upon your shores;
>   Put you not out to sea, lest it befall
>   That, losing me, yet should remain astray.[76]

He addresses only those who are hungry and thirsty for knowledge of God. "*In church with saints.*" All whom he meets in paradise are saints, naturally, and have only saintly interests. The only exception is where some one of them, having his thoughts recalled to earth by the mortal visitor, angrily vituperates mankind, or some part or person of mankind, for wickedness or folly. Abstract theology and brief lives of saints make up the burden of the talk. There are few interesting personalities introduced. The spirits whom Dante meets, reveal to him— and us—much of heaven and its laws and customs, but

[75] *Ib.*, iii.   [76] *Par.*, ii, 1–6.

little of themselves. By exception, indeed, Piccarda wins us by her sweet humility and by the pathos of her life-story. She, as Francesca, as Ugolino, rests her tale upon the unspoken. The tragic dénouement is hinted, not told: And Dante is never more "romantic" than in those three magic lines,—Francesca's

> "That day we read no farther in the book,"

Ugolino's

> "Then fasting was more powerful than grief,"

and Piccarda's

> "And God doth know what then my life became."

Piccarda is a lovely apparition, but for us as for Dante, shadowy as a pearl on a woman's white forehead. The sturdy ancient, Cacciaguida, contemner of his beloved city now enervate in luxury, is more humanly distinct,— especially for those unforgettable words foretelling the exile's woe—

> . . . how salt the taste
> Of others' bread, and how the path is hard
> Descending and ascending others' stairs.[77]

Vehement St. Peter also, in that tremendous indictment of his recreant successors, is true to the quick-tempered Disciple who in his righteous rage smote off the ear of the servant of Caiaphas. But the rest are little more than mouthpieces of information or wisdom.

Yet in spite of the abstract talk and the indistinct characters, the *Paradise* is far from being merely what is called a "metaphysical poem." Its total aesthetic appeal is more sensuous than that of either the *Hell* or the *Purgatory*. Dante has a difficult artistic problem. He must

[77] Par., xvii, 58–60.

paint everything in high light; there must be no shadows. To a certain extent, indeed, as we have seen, the physical shadow of the earth does reach out over the three lowest heavens, paling their light a little. But upward from the Sun, source of all physical light, we pass from sphere to sphere of supernal radiance more and more unendurably dazzling. So as she nears the Empyrean, blaze more consumingly Beatrice's smiling eyes. So increases the garmenting glory of the blessed spirits, colored like soft pearls, glowing topazes, flaming rubies. The several heavens are suffused with the tints of their planets,—with the silvery, mottled shimmer of the Moon, the golden incandescence of the Sun, the ruddy glow of Mars, the white purity of Saturn. Everywhere is loveliness of sound and movement. The rolling spheres themselves make a sweet harmony.[78] The spirits, wheeling and circling like luminous birds, carol, singly or in gracious accord or antiphony. Bouquets of delicious scent are they.[79] They group themselves into figures at once lovely and symbolic. Those of the Sun form a triple garland around Dante and Beatrice, like the halo on misty nights around the Moon.[80] Gabriel, circling over the head of Mary, so weaves a continuous crown of flame for that "beauteous sapphire of heaven."[81] Grouped into the shape of a white Cross against the blood-red Mars, the spirits course back and forth like moving torches behind alabaster, their voices rippling together like the strings of a harp.[82] The spirits of Jupiter prick in gold against silver their motto of Justice;[83] and themselves then outline a majestic Eagle, the bird of Jove. Their blended

[78] Par., i, 76–8. To gain this sensuous effect, Dante departs for once from his master, Aristotle, who repudiates Plato's "harmony of the spheres."

[79] Par., xix, 22–4.

[80] Ib., x.

[81] Ib., xxiii, 91 ff.

[82] Ib., xiv, 97 ff.

[83] Par., xix, 91–8.

speech is like the murmuring of a stream in its pebbly bed, or the sound "that shapeth in the lyre-neck, or in the joined pipes of an organ," or

> Like to the lark that goes her way in air,
> Singing at first, then silences her voice
> Content with her last sweetness satisfied.[84]

In Saturn we see, golden against the crystal candor of the planet, the mystic Ladder, thronged with splendors ascending and descending. In that contemplative heaven, there is a sudden aweing silence, broken as startlingly by the sudden thunder of a many-tongued cry.[85] Sensuously gorgeous again is the river of tawny light in the Empyrean, from which burst living sparks, that then bury themselves in the banking blossoms, "like rubies set in gold."[86] Like a stupendous pyrotechnic set-piece is the wheeling of the nine flaming angelic orders around that point of intolerable light from which "doth hang heaven and all nature."[87] Loveliest image of all is the Rose, which overcanopies the universe, and whose white petals spreading from a golden centre, form the thrones of the blest.[88] Finally, there rises before us the sensible image of the Trinity, bafflingly suggestive, gorgeous, of one dimension, yet of three colors,—white as snow, red as flame, green as emerald,—whose centre is the visible face of the human Christ.[89]

The most nearly perfect illustrator of the *Paradise* would have been, I think, Fra Angelico. He used the pigments Dante loved,—white and crusted gold, vivid red and blue and green. No doubt, Dante himself saw his saints and angels more as his contemporary, Giotto,

[84] *Ib.*, xx, 73–5.
[85] *Ib.*, xxi, 25–42; 139–42. Cf. *Rev.*, viii, 1.
[86] *Ib.*, xxx, 61 ff.   [87] *Ib.*, xxviii, 42.
[88] *Par.*, xxxi.   [89] *Ib.*, xxxiii.

would have drawn them. Dante too was something of a draughtsman. He tells in the New Life how visitors surprised him as he sat drawing an angel.[90] There can be little doubt that what he drew must have reminded us of the style of Giotto. Master-artists have always stamped their visual images upon their contemporaries, and for Dante Giotto was the supreme painter.[91] Nevertheless, Giotto could hardly have interpreted the imagery of the Paradise to us so sympathetically and convincingly as the defter, more mystical, Dominican. Botticelli's famous drawings, again, in their intricate beauty of line, suggest well the design and movement of Dante's picture, but besides the fatal lack of color, they have not the sensuous, yet mystical, tenderness, the austere winsomeness, that Fra Angelico knew how to express with pigments as Dante with words.

There is a touch of the childlike in the imagination of both. There is a childlike side to the gorgeousness of the Paradise, as there is to the gruesomeness of the Hell. One must be something of a child at heart to accept with unremitting seriousness the long-drawn-out pageant of whirling, circling, chanting choristers as at all a convincing picture of a credible or desirable after-life eternal. It is perhaps one proof of Dante's majestic and compelling personality that the Paradise has been rarely if ever parodied. Yet at times it calls upon all the courage of one's reverence.

To keep in full touch with the mood of the Divine Comedy, one must feel continually the symbol behind the fact. Such an image as the gigantic talking Eagle, for instance, is, apart from its symbolic meaning, rather a grotesque imagining. No doubt Dante visualized it not quite realistically, but as a schematic constellation. Indeed, nearly all the gyrations and groupings of the

[90] Ib., xxxv, 1–8.   [91] Purg., xi, 95.

162   **Dante**

flaming spirits of the *Paradise* suggest an astronomical
analogy as their source. Still, we accept the Eagle with
entire sympathy only when we realize intellectually its
meaningful fitness. Beatrice in the earthly paradise had
told Dante that he could not communicate to men her
transcendent truths as they were in themselves, but only
under images of sense.[92] She is more explicit as to this
language of "accommodation" in paradise. Dante, she
says, must remember that the appearance of the blessed
spirits in the several heavens, and their behavior there,
is but a kind of picture-language for his edification. They
do not really belong there, but in the immaterial, and
therefore unsensuous, Empyrean alone. A *fortiori*, their
behavior is representative of heavenly custom. But—

> Thus must your wit be spoken to, because
> Only through what is sensed it apprehends
> What it then makes worthy of intellect.
> On this account the Scripture condescends
> To your capacity, and feet and hands
> To God attributes, and means otherwise;
> And Holy Church in aspect like to men
> Gabriel and Michael represents to you,
> And him who made Tobias whole again.[93]

Relatively to angelic intelligence, human wit is indeed a
childish thing. And so one may say that Dante finds philosophical justification for the childlike aspect of his art.
It is as if he applied to the readers of his *Paradise* the
text,—"Except ye be converted, and become as little
children, ye shall not enter into the kingdom of heaven."
And he several times compares himself to a little child.

Yet we must be knowing children, too. To recur to the
Eagle, we must catch the fitness of the classic "bird of
Jove" appearing in the sphere named after him. We
must recall, as is indeed easy after Justinian's narra-

[92] Purg., xxxiii, 76–8.   [93] Par., iv, 40–48.

tive,[94] the divinely ordained triumph of the Roman Eagle, and so realize the inevitableness of the king of birds
symbolizing Temporal Justice. And as Justice is the highest moral virtue, we are led to remember also that other
golden-plumed Eagle which upraised the dreaming Dante
to a fire in which both he and it were consumed.[95] For,
as I have suggested, this Eagle probably intends the
divine spark in the soul which kindles it to virtue, where-
by it is raised at last to the Empyrean, or "heaven of
fire," in which moral virtue is transcended. Already
Aquinas had likened this divine "spark" to an eagle.
Thus an image, which as a pure object of sense seems
naïvely crude, takes on for the understanding a rich significance and poetic dignity.

This interpenetration of the sensuous and the significant is perhaps the dominant virtue of Dante's art. He
holds with Keats that "beauty is truth, truth beauty,"
but only if both coexist in one representation. Beauty
without intellectual significance, beauty as mere orna-
ment, he contemns. In art, as in doctrine, he holds to
the principle of "economy." It is therefore ironic that
there are certain modern critics who would reject as val-
ueless Dante's "truth," and yet hope to retain his
"beauty." Dante is tolerant; he has in fact made his poetry say to them—

"Give heed at least how beautiful I am;"

but he has also characterized them as persons not "bene
accorte,"—persons not of deep insight.

By way of conclusion, however, we may consider this
modern attitude towards Dante more closely.

[94] Par., vi.   [95] Purg., ix, 19–31.

CONCLUSION

Conclusion

THE greatest poet of modern Italy, Giosué Carducci, has packed into a remarkable sonnet his total evaluation of Dante. I translate the sense of his sonnet without hope of reproducing its chiseled beauty.

> Dante, how comes it that I, reverent, bear
> Such votive homage to thy shrine sublime?
> That me the sun leaves bending o'er the rhyme
> That made thee gaunt, and dawn still finds me there?
>
> For me St. Lucy prays not, nor the fair
> Matilda laves away my spirit's grime,
> And Beatrice and her chaste lover climb
> Godward in vain along the starry stair.
>
> I hate thy Holy Empire; and my sword
> I would from thy good Frederick's head had cleft
> The crown, when he in Val d'Olona warred.
>
> Empire and Church are ruins life-bereft,
> Whence soars thy song, unto the skies outpoured:
> Jove passes,—and the poet's hymn is left.

More recently, George Santayana has rendered a similar judgment in a more broadly philosophical way. "A thousand years after Homer, Alexandrian critics were expounding his charming myths as if they were a revealed treatise of physics and morals. A thousand years after Dante we may hope that his conscientious vision of the universe, where all is love, magic, and symbolism, may charm mankind exclusively as poetry."[1]

In such event, it was with good reason that Dante thanked Virgil for his "fair style," for there would appear to be nothing else left to do him honor. His poetry must cry out,—not because we are inacapable of understanding its message, but because we understand and reject that message:

"Give heed at least how beautiful I am."

What do they mean, these critics? Is it anything like what Lowell meant when he said of Edmund Spenser,— "The true use of him is as a gallery of pictures which we visit as the mood takes us"? If so be, "to what base uses we may return!" For such use of a consummate poet were but a child's use,—or an aesthete's, more childish than a child's.

I am confident that when Mr. Santayana says he would have Dante's "vision of the universe" "charm mankind exclusively as poetry," he means a good deal by "poetry." Yet I do not like his word "charm." I recall Horace's—

Omne tulit punctum qui miscuit utile dulci
Lectorem delectando, pariterque monendo.

To say that Dante properly should "charm" us seems— perhaps unintentionally—to imply ex silentio that he can

[1] Three Philosophical Poets, Cambridge, 1910, pp. 103–4.

do nothing else, that he has not "mixed the useful with the sweet," that he can still be "delectable" to the reader, but no longer "instructive," that in fine he may offer us beauty but not wisdom.

Naturally, I would not use Mr. Santayana as a stalking-horse unfairly. It would be impossible here to do justice to his whole judgment of Dante. The words I have quoted from his essay, however, at least by themselves indicate—like Carducci's sonnet—a limitation of our interest in Dante unfair to him and to ourselves. He should mean vastly more to us, I think, than a master of a delectable style or a thing of quotable shreds and purple patches. Either he has wisdom to offer us in beauty, or he has not. In the latter case, surely his poetry is like the Siren he dreamed of on purgatory-mount, outwardly fair, but inwardly false.

Now much of Dante's teaching is false. We may be forced to agree with Santayana that "Dante's idea of nature is not genuine; it is not sincerely put together out of reasoned observation. It is a view of nature intercepted by myths and worked out by dialectic.[2] And we must agree with the consequent charge that "the higher philosophy is not safe if the lower philosophy is wanting." Indeed, in his pitiless logic Mr. Santayana would drive us still farther. That false view of nature vitiates for him even Dante's poetry,—that poetry which was to endure a thousand years to charm mankind. Thanks to this false natural philosophy, "there is," he says, "an attenuated texture and imagery in the *Divine Comedy*. The voice that sings it, from beginning to end, is a thin boy-treble, all wonder and naïveté. This art does not smack of life, but of somnambulism."

One begins to feel that there is being proved too much. Our concessions seem to have landed us in mere para-

[2] *Op. cit.*, p. 208.

dox. If to the philosopher, Dante's voice sounds like "a thin boy-treble," we may feel reasonably certain that there is something wrong with the philosopher's hearing.

The retort is not merely flippant. The trouble, I venture to think, with Mr. Santayana's damaging indictment of Dante's criticism of life is that he hears it too exclusively as a system, whether of natural or moral philosophy. He fails apparently to take into account the wide and deep knowledge of men and things that Dante gained from experience. That is what tells, and teaches. Out of the depth and breadth of his living, out of his loves and hates, his hopes and despairs, his laughter and tears, was built up his personality,—a personality that spoke no "thin boy-treble," if we may trust any portrait of him, or any contemporary testimony. I have taken exception to some things that Carlyle read out of the Bargello portrait. What was really before Carlyle's mind's eye was rather the visage of the older Dante, gaunt and life-scarred, truly "an altogether tragic, heart-affecting face." Carlyle was surely in the main right. It is not the face of a "somnambulist," seeing life dimly as through a dream. It is, to use a phrase of Byron's, the face of one foremost among the

Men of the world who know the world like men.

Such knowledge of the world is real knowledge. It is not rendered nugatory because its possessor happens to entertain scientific theories that have given way to others, themselves probably also impermanent, and opinions upon the temporal welfare and ultimate destiny of man which some of us cannot share. Intellectual systems, whether physical or metaphysical, are but strings of the mind with which we tie up the *data* of experience into convenient packages. We are forever cutting the old strings, and rearranging our packages. But the real value is not in the wrapping, but in the experience contained. So, conceding that the medieval wrappings of Dante's experience of life have grown mouldy, may we not cut them away, and yet enquire what there may be still vital in that experience itself? Having elsewhere attempted in a small way an answer to this question, perhaps I may be permitted to refer to that essay, and to digest here some portions of it.[3]

The greatest upset in human opinion that has happened since Dante's time is, I conceive, the substitution of the Copernican system of astronomy for the Ptolemaic. Also, the triumph of the new astronomy involved the greatest defeat ever suffered by human pride. Hitherto the universe had revolved about man; now man went spinning somewhere in the bleak outerness. In the picturesque phrase of Professor Royce's, the earth was forthwith reduced to a "mere local item in the news of the universe." Yet though true from the standpoint of the citizens of heaven, the statement is hardly true for those of earth. However much humbler his habitation, there is still nothing more interesting for mankind than man. Indeed, like all suburbanites, we residents of this now out-of-the-way planet are only the more thrown back upon ourselves and our own resources. Cut off—for our mortal lives at least—from cosmopolitan activities and the courts of heaven, we must needs make the most of our local, our earthly selves. Amidst all the modern varieties of belief and unbelief, there is the one practical agreement that our present task as men is the betterment of human conditions. We are at least bound to make ours the "suburb beautiful." For us, more emphatically even than for the philosopher recorded by Pliny, "God is the helping of man by man."

[3] *The Modernness of Dante. Anniversary Papers by Colleagues and Pupils of George Lyman Kittredge.* Boston, 1913.

And this is just what Dante is forever saying and explaining and illustrating. That in his theology, God is also a real and transcendent Being, is a quite detachable idea, which, if we like, we may ignore altogether.

In his essay on *Monarchy*, which is really a discussion of the whole right governance of man on this earth, Dante lays down as a starting-point the thesis: "The work proper to the human race, taken as a whole, is to keep the whole capacity of the potential intellect constantly actualized, primarily for speculation, and secondarily (by extension and for the sake of the other) for action."[4] Translated into modern language, this fundamental ideal of life differs in no essential from such modern teaching as that, say, of Matthew Arnold. "Speculation," as the outcome of keeping "the whole capacity of the potential intellect constantly actualized," is, so far as human experience is concerned, not really different from what Arnold means by culture,—"culture being," to quote his familiar words, "a pursuit of our total perfection by means of getting to know, on all the matters which most concern us, the best which has been thought and said in the world." Arnold would give three-fifths of life to conduct; Dante would apparently give three-fifths to "speculation." We need not quarrel about the odd one-fifth. The important thing is that the Florentine no less than the Victorian is asserting that the goal of humanity is more humanity, not any medieval stifling of the life that is in us, but rational enlargement of that life, more and "new life" on earth in "sweetness and light."

And to this end, this "greatest good" on earth, continues the author of the essay on *Monarchy*, the primary condition is peace. "In the quiet or tranquillity of peace, the human race is most freely and favorably disposed towards the work proper to it." But to be efficient to its

4 I, iv, 1–5.

end, this peaceful work must be organized, must have
unity of direction. So Dante argues for an international
tribunal to keep the peace and to direct the coöperation
of men towards the realization of fullest humanity. Dante
postulated for his international tribunal a world emperor
at Rome; we a world parliament at the Hague.

We have grown democratic. It may perhaps be said
that just there rises a barrier between Dante and us. His
world is a world of caste, a social hierarchy as stiffly
ringed and graded as his immutable hell. He lacks sympathy with man as man. Whether in hell or heaven, he
will converse only with people of importance in their
day, and takes an almost exclusive interest in "good society." The great revolutionary watchwords of modern
democracy—liberty, equality, fraternity—are not heard
in a state so rigidly policed by prince and priest. It is on
such indictment that the democratic Carducci rejected
all in Dante but his "poetry."

Well, as to equality, Dante certainly does not believe,
in any romantically literal sense, that men are born
equal. No one does, or ever did—really. Nature opposes
too obvious a veto. But apart from Nature's favoritism,
inequality is essential to human progress itself. For human progress demands social organization; social organization involves diversity of individual function,—which
is to say, speaking plainly, humble jobs as well as exalted jobs, privates as well as captains, stokers as well
as stewards, college professors as well as college presi-
dents,—or in a word, inequality.

We of to-day realize these natural and necessary limitations of the gospel of equality more fully than did
our more revolutionary and romantic grandfathers and
great-grandfathers. And the words which Dante puts into
the mouth of the young Charles Martel in paradise reach
over to us with singular intimacy. "Would it be worse

for man on earth were he no citizen,"—that is, were he
not a member of organized society? And when Dante
agrees that it would, Charles is ready with just the argument we should make. "And may that be," he asks,
"except men live below diversely and with diverse offices?" As modernly, Charles protests against the very
basis of medieval caste when he denies place or office to
hereditary right. A man is indeed born, if you will, to his
office, his place in society, but—not because he is his
father's son. Personal fitness, inborn merit, alone should
qualify him for his birthright.

> But to religion ye turn him aside
>   Born to be girded with a sword; and him
>   Who is a man for preaching ye make king;
> So that your track is outside of the road.[5]

In the true sense of the word, Dante does not seem to
be so undemocratic, after all.

And again what a richly democratic ideal is implied in
the single line that, fully understood, contains Dante's
whole philosophy of love,—

> Love and the gentle heart are one same thing![6]

We have seen how Dante continued and developed
Guinicelli's transformation of the Provençal troubadour's
socially genteel into the spiritually gentle, and the loving-
service of an aristocratic lady into loving-service of God
and one's fellowmen. If love is thus measure of gentility,
of station and office, and if love is self-devoted service,
then Dante's practical solution of social inequality becomes plain. It is for the general good that the right man
should be in the right place, and the right kind of man,
the gentleman, will cheerfully acquiesce in his place, be
it high or low. All that he, as one moved wholly by love,

[5] Par., viii, 145–8.   [6] New Life, son. x, 1.

asks for is greatest possible serviceableness. To be doing
what one is qualified for doing, to be where one service-
ably belongs—that is the basis for content, the necessary
condition for inward peace. And the inward peace of each
is as essential for the general good as the outward peace
of all. So the meek Piccarda expresses to Dante her contentment with her place in the lowly heaven of the Moon.

> Brother, virtue of charity doth put
>   Our will to rest, and make us only wish
>   For what we have, and thirst for naught beside.
> If we desired to have a higher place,
>   Then our desires would be discordant from
>   The will of Him who bids us here abide. . . .
> And His will is our peace.[7]

Piccarda's mood is emphatically not mere reluctant res-
ignation to God's will. She has come to understand what
all men on earth should understand, that the aspiration
to highest service is quite a different thing from the aspiration to higher place. Incompetent to a higher place,
she would be of less service in it. Now in her right place,
all her powers have full play. From no one can more be
asked; to no one can more be given. "Perfect service is
perfect freedom."

For human conduct the moral of Piccarda's words is
obvious. They do not spell for us "quietism" or "stand-
pattism," or exalt the maxim "Whatever is, is best."
Personal ambition, the desire to better oneself in the
world, is justifiable so long as one's power for good measures up to the coveted place. For the individual as well
as for the race it is right that "the whole capacity of the
potential intellect" should be kept "constantly actualized." Else there is waste. So anyone who sincerely feels
that he has not found or been allotted his right place, his

---

[7] Par., iii, 70–5, 85.

place of greatest usefulness, has a right, nay, a duty to protest. Not only he but, through him, society is the loser by the dislocation. "Noble discontent" is awakened when one is needlessly kept from doing one's best. But individual discontent or social unrest, when stirred by desire of self-aggrandizement and not of disinterested service, is like the ambition of the bullfrog in the fable to swell himself to the bigness of the bull. His was not "noble discontent"; it merely—as the event proved—spoiled a "perfectly good" frog. We may heroically resolve to hitch our wagon to a star; but we should remember that such a team calls for a specially gifted driver.

To proclaim a natural inequality adapted to social need; a social justice bent on giving each individual, regardless of his social antecedents, his fullest scope, and so his greatest opportunity and reward of service; an individual and collective service wholly dedicated and efficiently controlled to the realization of human perfection, full actualization of the whole potential capacity of mankind for speculation and action; liberty, equality, fraternity interpreted essentially in the spirit of the twentieth century—to proclaim such a program with clarity and beauty of utterance is more than to "charm mankind exclusively as poetry." Veiled, if you will, with "myth" and "magic," Dante's message is still prophetic. If indeed a "somnambulist," he was one that walked, as Horace said, "post mediam noctem quum somnia vera."

And yet, when all is said, for all the beauty and wisdom of Dante's poetry, he makes to us, I believe, a yet more compelling appeal. I mean through his personality itself. Truly, as Carlyle says, "Great Men, taken up in any way, are profitable company." There is truth also in his statement that "true souls, in all generations of the world, who look on this Dante, will find a brotherhood in him; the deep sincerity of his thoughts, his woes and hopes, will speak likewise to their sincerity; they will feel that this Dante too was a brother."[8] Yet, in frankness, it is hardly a feeling of intimacy, of "brotherhood," that I feel in the presence of Dante, but rather a sense of awe and humility. As an artist, he may charm; as a teacher, instruct and enlighten; as a man, he is by no means always admirable, but he is always, and above all things, lordly. He rises, like Farinata in hell,

> upright with breast and countenance,
> As if he entertained great scorn of hell.

To his contemporaries, Dante's "disdainful spirit" was intimidating. He remains so still, and to those who love and admire him most. One would like to have talked with Shakspere; only greatness itself—or impudence—could have been at ease with Dante. But to feel small before true lordliness of character is medicinal for the soul. "Serve the great," exclaims Emerson. "Stick at no humiliation. Grudge no office thou canst render. Be the limb of their body, the breath of their mouth. Compromise thy egotism. Who cares for that, so thou gain aught wider and nobler."[9]

[8] *The Hero as Poet.*
[9] *Representative Men,* Lect. I.

Index

179